The Playbook

39 Short Skits for ESL, High School, or Adult Students

Tim McDaniel

Bookasaurus Publishing
607 H Street Ne
Auburn, WA 98002

©Copyright 2020 by Tim McDaniel.
First Edition.
ISBN: 9781660908783

All rights reserved. All rights, including professional, motion picture, radio broadcasting, television, video or sound taping, all other forms of mechanical or electronic reproductions such as information storage and retrieval systems and photocopying, and the rights of translations into foreign languages, are strictly reserved by the publisher, Bookasaurus Publishing. Any inquiries concerning these rights should be directed to the publisher (address given above).

The rights to unlimited amateur productions of these plays at one location are granted with the publication of this book.

Permission to reproduce copies of the plays included in this text is granted to amateur groups and educational institutions with the purchase of this book. All copies must display the copyright notice indicated on this page. Copies of these plays and amateur performance rights are for the purchaser and purchasing organization only. These rights may not be sold or transferred to any third party.

NOTICE FOR PROFESSIONAL PRODUCTION
For any form of non-amateur presentation (professional stage, radio, video, or television), permission must be obtained in writing from the publisher, Bookasaurus Publishing (address above).

Front Cover Image by Gerd Altmann from Pixaby

Note to the Teacher or Director:

This collection came about because I was assigned to teach a combined-level (Levels 1 – 3, in our Intensive English Program) course that included Drama as a major component. Preparing for the course, I located many interesting exercises and role-play scenarios, but I was disappointed when I searched for collections of suitable skits.

The collections I examined were too low, or too high, for my students. Or they focused on grammatical structures or vocabulary – at the expense of a fun story, in my opinion. Or they presupposed a knowledge of American customs and attitudes that my students might not have. Or they dealt with situations that my students would have a hard time relating to.

Finally I stopped looking, and decided to write my own skits. Although I have long been a writer of short stories (mostly fantasy and science fiction), I had never done anything like this project before. However, I found it a lot of fun.

While writing the skits I have tried to keep the language fairly simple, and the characters fairly broad types, to help my students understand and more fully enter the situations and stories.

I have not included much in the way of stage directions, as I feel that the directors, teachers, and students will derive a deeper understanding of the material if they have to think for themselves about the characters' tones, emotions, body language, and movements.

I think it is important to note that the genders of most or all of the characters in the skits can be altered, depending on the wishes of the teachers/directors and the actors. Names can similarly be changed, if the students find them hard to pronounce or have unfortunate connotations. The skits are yours to play with – change whatever you want to change!

A companion book to the one you are holding with ancillary materials with pre-reading questions, staging notes, a language focus for each skit, post reading discussion questions, and post-performance discussion questions, is currently being prepared, and may be already available to you, depending on when you are reading this. I did not include these materials in the present volume, as I thought it would make the book too long. (However, the ancillary materials books will be considerably cheaper!)

Finally, I would love to hear your comments on the skits, and how well they work with your actors. (You can contact me at ajaantim19@gmail.com.) My students have been performing these skits for several quarters, and they seem to enjoy them – how about yours? I would be interested in any suggestions your have, also, for any future editions of the book. And, of course, I would greatly appreciate any reviews you can give this book on Amazon or elsewhere.

Tim McDaniel
January 2020

Note to the Student/Actor:

If you have not acted before, it can be scary. You may feel that the people in the audience are just waiting for you to make a mistake so they can laugh at you or pity you.

That's wrong.

People in the audience want to have a good time, and so they want you to succeed. They understand that it is hard to be on stage, and they are rooting for you to do a good job. And guess what? They'll forgive you if make a mistake!

Ask yourself: if YOU were in the audience, watching a play, would YOU be waiting for the actors to make a mistake so you can laugh at them? Of course not. So the people watching you feel the same way.

And here is a secret: the people watching your play don't know the play as well as you do. They won't know if you change a word here or there. They won't know if you forgot to do some action that you planned to do.

So just have fun. Yes, it's a lot of work. Acting takes a lot of practice. You will have to spend a lot of time memorizing your part. It will take time to figure out how to make the play as good as you can – how loudly you should speak, where you should stand, what kinds of movement you should make, what your tone of voice should be. But even though it is a lot of work, you can do it. Your fellow actors and your director are all there to help you.

And when you finish, and the audience applauds – that's a great feeling!

Tim McDaniel
January 2020

Table of Contents

Wake Up 1
The Lonely Hearts Club 7
The Other Woman 13
The Bad Tattoo 18
First Week 23
Can I Pass? 30
The Diamond Job 36
Detectives 41
The Ghosts 45
Cleaning Up 51
The Cheaters 57
The New Teacher 62
Vampire Hunters 67
At the Restaurant 73
Time for Love 80
Why I Need More Money 88
Psychiatric Help 5¢ 98
Vacation Plans 106
Star-Crossed Lovers 111
Dreams Come True 119

Five Easy Dollars	125
iPhone, uPhone	131
Soldiers and Spies	135
Doctor's Waiting Room	141
An Unforgettable Wedding	147
Ups and Downs	153
The Robot's Purpose	159
The Doctors	166
Three Wishes	172
The Case of the Missing Bicycle	178
First Contact	182
Zombie Invasion	189
The Race	195
The Messy Operation	199
Better Late than Never	207
Gunslingers	214
Freeze Ray!	220
Only Robots	225
The Landing Party	231
Appendix: Summaries and Difficulty Levels	238

Wake Up

CAST:

Sleeper: Sue
Friend 1: Ralph
Friend 2: Enid
Friend 3: Drew

SETTING: School lunchroom

(Ralph, Enid, and Drew are already at a table; a sleepy Sue walks past them.)

Ralph: Hey, Sue! Come join us! There's lots of room!

(Sue sits with them.)

Hey, you said yesterday you had a math quiz this morning. How did it go? Was it hard?

Enid: Don't ask her. She doesn't know. She didn't come to class until the quiz was over!

Ralph: Oh? Where were you?

Sue: Sleeping. I was sleepy this morning, and I couldn't get out of bed on time.

Drew: Don't you have an alarm clock? Or you can set an alarm on your phone.

Sue: I have an alarm.

Drew: Maybe it wasn't loud enough.

Sue: It woke me up. But then I just turned it off and fell asleep again.

Enid: Last year I had trouble getting out of bed. I put my alarm on a chair on the other side of the room. That way, I had to get out of bed to turn it off.

Sue: Even if I get up, I fall asleep again. Sometimes I fall asleep while I am eating breakfast. One time I fell asleep in the shower.

Ralph: Oh, that's too bad. I have an idea! I can call you every morning, and make sure you are awake. Just give me your phone number.

Sue: How would that be different from an alarm? It won't work.

Ralph: Oh. Well, you could give me your phone number anyway, if you want.

(Sue puts her head on the table)

Drew: They should make alarm clocks that shoot cold water at you, or something like that.

Enid: And then your bed would be wet.

Drew: Have you tried putting cold water on your face, Sue?

Ralph: Shhh. She's sleeping.

Enid: Wake up!

Sue: Huh?

Enid: You had better eat your lunch. We don't have a long lunch break.

Sue: Oh, yeah.

Drew: Wow, you really do need to find a way to wake up.

Ralph:	I could come to your house every morning, and bring you a nice cup of coffee from Starbucks.
Enid:	Or you could try one of those energy drinks.
Sue:	Energy drinks?
Enid:	Yeah, like Red Bull or Monster. They have a lot of caffeine.
Drew:	But I heard those drinks are bad for you. They have a lot of caffeine, but they also have a lot of sugar.
Sue:	Well, I don't want a lot of sugar! I don't want to get fat.
Ralph:	Don't worry. You look great. But if you don't want to use those energy drinks, remember I can bring you coffee.
Sue:	Oh, that's not fair to you. You would have to get up really early.
Ralph:	I don't mind!
Sue:	No, I'm sure I can find a better way.
Enid:	You could get a thermos.
Sue:	What's a thermos?
Enid:	You know, one of those metal cans. They keep your drink hot for a long time. I have one in my bag. See?
Ralph:	Yeah. My mom has one of those.
Enid:	You could put some hot coffee in the thermos, and then you could have hot coffee in the morning.
Drew:	Can it really keep the coffee hot all night?
Sue:	I bet I would forget to put coffee in the thermos, anyway.

Drew: Maybe you could pay someone to slap your face every ten minutes. Like this.

(Drew lightly taps Sue's face. Sue brushes the hand away.)

That will keep you from falling asleep, right?

Ralph: Don't hurt her.

Drew: I didn't slap her hard.

Ralph: Are you OK, Sue?

Sue: Yeah, I'm fine. I just don't know what I can do. Enid:

Doctors say we need eight hours of sleep every night.

Ralph: And they also say that teenagers need even more than that. Like about ten hours or something.

Sue: There's no way I can get ten hours of sleep at night! School starts too early!

Drew: Some schools are starting later, to give students more time to sleep.

Enid: But not our school.

Drew: Yeah.

(Sue stands up and starts to walk around, slapping her face.)

Sue: So what can I do? Come on, guys! Give me some more ideas! I can't keep sleeping in class!

Enid: I don't know, Sue. We talked about alarm clocks, and cold water, and asking someone to call you, and coffee –

Ralph: I still think the best idea is for me to bring you coffee every morning.

Enid:	Yeah, yeah. And energy drinks, and slapping. I can't think of anything else you can do.
Sue:	Oh, it's terrible! I'm going to fail my classes!
Drew:	I wish we had some other ideas. Sorry.
Ralph:	Maybe we'll think of something later. Hey, what are you going to do after school today, Sue?
	(Sue sits down again.)
Sue:	My homework. But after dinner I'm going to a movie with Jane and Kris.
Ralph:	Oh? What time? Maybe if I'm not busy, I could come, too.
Sue:	The movie starts at ten.
Ralph:	Ten? At night? That's pretty late.
Sue:	Yeah. And then after the movie we're going to a coffee shop. It should be fun.
Ralph:	So what time do you think you will get back home?
Sue:	Well, the movie ends about midnight, and then we'll go to the coffee shop, so probably I will get home about two or three. Maybe four.
Enid:	That's a late night!
Drew:	Yeah. I can't stay up that late.
Ralph:	I guess I can't stay up that late, either. If I don't go to bed before midnight, I am always too sleepy the next day at school.
Sue:	Oh, that's too bad. Oh, well. Maybe you can come with us another time. I got to go now, guys. See you!
Drew:	Don't sleep in class!

Enid: See you!

(Sue leaves.)

Ralph: Did you hear that? Maybe I can go out with her another time!

Enid: Oh, Ralph, you are so stupid. You could go on a date with her tonight. What's the problem with staying up late? Staying up late never hurt anyone. Why not stay up late?

The Lonely Hearts Club

CAST:

Aleesa
Ethan
Brad
Joy

SETTING: A meeting room

> *(Aleesa arrives, and puts chairs in a circle, and puts out some cookies. She waits nervously. The others arrive.)*

Aleesa: Hi, everyone! Welcome! Please, have a seat. See? I put them in a circle. Wasn't that a good idea? And I brought cookies. Nice, right? Please, sit down!

Ethan: *(Takes a bite out of a cookie.)* These cookies are terrible. Maybe you should learn to cook.

Aleesa: Oh, well, others really like them. They say they are great cookies, so I don't know. Anyway, hi, everyone! Welcome! Welcome to the first meeting of the Broken Hearts Club!

Brad: Hi. I was cutting the grass in my yard, and then I checked the mail, but I didn't get any letters. Then I came here.

Joy: That's a really exciting story. NOT!

Ethan: No wonder you can't get anyone to date you. You're really boring.

Aleesa: Well, that's why we are here, right? I mean, none of us are getting any dates, so I set up this club so we could have a good time, anyway! Good idea, right?

Joy: Yeah, a great idea. NOT!

Ethan: That's getting really annoying.

Brad: One time something happened to me that was really annoying. But I don't remember what it was. It was really annoying, though.

Aleesa: Well, my idea – and I think it's a really great idea – is that we have our meetings, and have a good time together, and then we will be happy people. And then people will want to date us. Good idea, right? It's MY idea! I thought it up!

Joy: Oh, yeah – a great idea. Ha!

Ethan: That's not going to work, you know.

Aleesa: Why not?

Ethan: Look, why don't people want to date you? It's because you only talk about yourself all the time!

Aleesa: I don't just talk about myself! I talk about lots of things! Everyone says I talk about a lot of things!

Ethan: Just about yourself. And look at Brad. He's Mr. Boring! He is so boring he probably makes all the girls fall asleep when he starts talking!

Brad: I can talk about sleep. I went to bed about ten o'clock last night. No, actually it was about ten-fifteen. I remember it was dark outside, and I felt sleepy, so I said, "I'm going to go to bed." And I did. I slept all night. I don't remember my dreams.

Ethan: See how boring he is?

Joy: Oh, he's not boring! Oh –wait a minute – yes, he IS! Ethan:

And you – you think you're funny. You're not funny at all.

Joy:	Well, shut up, then.
Aleesa:	OK, Ethan, so what about you? You can tell everyone else why they are not popular, but what about you? You can't get a date, either!
Ethan:	No, I can't. It's because I am a jerk.
Brad:	A jerk?
Ethan:	Yeah. I'm not nice. I'm not friendly. I'm not nice to anyone.
Joy:	Oh, really? You seem so nice to everyone. Not! I'm kidding. You're a number-one jerk, for sure.
Aleesa:	So that is why I had the wonderful idea to start this club! None of us can get dates, but we can hang out with each other and have a good time.
Brad:	Well, I came to the meeting because I had nothing else to do. Maybe I could watch TV or sit on the couch, I guess. Eat some potato chips. I like potato chips, but not all the time.
Aleesa:	Well, OK. So, Joy – why did YOU come to the meeting?
Joy:	Because it's, like SO much fun. Right.
Aleesa:	How about you? Well, Ethan?
Ethan:	Well, what?
Aleesa:	Why did you come?
Ethan:	I don't know. I saw Joy coming this way, so I thought, why not.
Joy:	You came because I was coming here? I was just walking this way, and I saw you, and I came in here. I thought this was where you were going.
Ethan:	So – you were following me?
Joy:	More like you were following me. Duh.

Ethan: But why? Why were you following me?

Joy: Like you don't know.

Ethan: Know what?

Joy: That you're so cute. Duh.

Ethan: Yeah, right. You're the cute one.

Joy: Really?

Ethan: Duh.

Aleesa: Isn't this nice? We formed the club to help us not be so lonely, and look! We have a new couple now! This is so sweet. My idea was so good. Don't you think?

Ethan: Shut up. It's not like that.

Joy: Yeah. Maybe Ethan is going to be your boyfriend. Not!

Ethan: Ha! You're really funny.

Aleesa: Well, I think it's sweet. What do you think, Brad?

Brad: I agree with whatever you want to say. I mean, there are many kinds of sweet, right? There's candy, ice cream, cake, pie, sugar, love, puppies, stuff like that. I love candy. Last night—

(Ethan and Joy whisper to each other during this conversation.)

Aleesa: OK, Brad. You can be quiet.

Brad: Sure.

Ethan: Hey, so Joy and I are going to go to a movie.

Joy: Yeah. You guys can come, too. Kidding! No way can you come!

Ethan: You're really funny! Anyway, you guys can stay in your losers' club. We're leaving.

Aleesa:	Bye! Have fun! I'm glad my idea helped you so much!
	(Ethan and Joy leave, hand in hand.)
	I think it's so sweet they are a couple. They won't be lonely anymore. I bet they are so happy that I made this club. They probably want to thank me. It was a really good idea.
Brad:	Yeah. I have an idea, too.
Aleesa:	What?
Brad:	I think that you are sweet, too. I mean, it's great you think about other people all the time.
Aleesa:	Yeah, isn't that good of me!
Brad:	I remember one time, I had this idea, and I—
Aleesa:	Brad.
Brad:	Yeah?
Aleesa:	Be quiet.
Brad:	OK.
Aleesa:	Wow – you know, you're a really good listener.
Brad:	You're a good talker.
Aleesa:	Do you want to be my boyfriend? I think we could be a good couple.
Brad:	Yeah, OK. Maybe after the meeting we could have dinner. Sometimes I cook dinner. Last night I made spaghetti. It was OK, but—
Aleesa:	Brad?
Brad:	Yeah?
Aleesa:	Be quiet.

Brad: OK.

Aleesa: Yeah, this is really nice. Come on, Brad. Let's go. You can make me dinner.

Brad: OK.

(Aleesa and Brad leave, hand in hand.)

The Other Woman

CAST:

	Jenny
Jenny's Friend:	Gabby
Jenny's Boyfriend:	Brad
	Orlando

Gabby: Hi, Jenny!

Jenny: Oh, hi, Gabby.

Gabby: So – what's new?

Jenny: Oh, nothing much.

Gabby: Hey – did you hear about Joy? My friend Alvin told me he saw Joy steal some candy from the store!

Jenny: Gabby, I don't want to hear any gossip, OK? You always have stories about all of our friends. I don't think it's nice.

Gabby: Well, OK, if you don't want to hear the news.

Jenny: I don't.

Gabby: Then I guess you don't want to hear the news about your boyfriend. His name is Bran, right?

Jenny: Brad, not Bran.

Gabby: Oh, Brad. So you don't want to hear about who Brad was with at the movie theater last night?

Jenny: Brad didn't go to the movies last night. He had a lot of homework. He told me.

Gabby: Oh – did his homework have long, blonde hair?

Jenny: What are you talking about?

Gabby: Jackie went the movies last night, and she said she saw Brad – your boyfriend – with another girl.

Jenny: Another girl? I don't believe it. Brad would never do that to me.

Gabby: Maybe you just don't want to know the truth.

Jenny: What truth? Brad was doing homework last night.

Gabby: Oh, yeah. I am sure Brad likes doing homework instead of going to a movie with a cute girl with long, blonde hair.

Jenny: I don't believe you.

Gabby: Jackie saw them. Oh – look! Here comes Brad now!

(Brad enters.)

Gabby: Hi, Brad.

Brad: Hi, Gabby. Hi, Jenny! How's it going?

Jenny: Fine, I guess.

Gabby: Don't act so nice around Jenny, Brad. She knows.

Brad: Huh?

Jenny: Oh, Gabby, be quiet.

Gabby: She knows about your new girlfriend.

Brad: What are you talking about?

Gabby: The girl you went to the movie with last night.

Brad: I didn't go to a movie. I was playing video games with some friends.

Jenny: Video games? You told me you had to do homework!

Brad: Well, I did, but then, uh—

Gabby: You see, Jenny? He's such a liar.

Brad: I am not a liar!

Jenny: Then why did you tell me you had to do homework?

Brad: I just didn't want you to feel bad. Because I wanted to play with some friends.

Gabby: One special friend, right? A girl with long blonde hair?

Brad: No!

Jenny: You have to tell me the truth, Brad.

Brad: I did! I mean, yeah, I lied a little bit about the homework, but now I am telling you the truth!

Jenny: I don't know if I can trust you.

Brad: You can! You can trust me!

Gabby: Why should she trust a liar?

Jenny: Did you go to a movie with another girl, or not?

Brad: I didn't! I was playing with some friends!

Gabby: Look – there's Orlando. He's one of your friends, right?

Brad: Yeah, but—

Jenny: Let's ask him where you were! Hey, Orlando?

(Orlando enters.)

Orlando: Hey, everyone. Hi, Brad. What's up?

Jenny: Did you, or did you not, play video games with Brad last night?

Brad: You don't understand. He—

Jenny: I'm asking Orlando, Brad! Well?

Orlando: Last night? No, I wasn't playing video games.

Gabby: Ah, hah!

Jenny: Oh, Brad! I can't believe you lied to me!

Brad: I didn't lie! I mean, except for the first time.

Orlando: I was going to go to Brad's house to play video games, but then my roommate introduced me to his sister. A really cute girl, with long, blonde hair. So I asked her to go to a movie, and we did!

Jenny: So YOU were the guy that went out with a blonde girl last night? Not Brad?

Orlando: No, Brad was at home playing video games with Tony and John.

Jenny: Oh, Brad! I'm so sorry that I thought you were cheating!

Brad: Well, it's all right now, anyway.

Jenny: And you, Gabby, were spreading gossip!

Gabby: It's not my fault! Jackie told me that she saw them at the theater!

Orlando: Who's Jackie?

Brad: I don't know Jackie, either.

Jenny: She's Gabby's friend. She's really tall, with red hair.

Orlando: Oh – I don't know her, but a tall, redheaded girl was giving me weird looks at the theater.

Jenny:	Because she thought you were Brad.
Brad:	And then she gossiped to Gabby—
Orlando:	And Gabby gossiped to you— Jenny:
	And caused all this trouble!
Gabby:	I'm so sorry! I'll try to control myself next time.
Brad:	Well, at least everything is OK, now. I have to go. Jenny – see you later?
Jenny:	Sure.
Orlando:	I got to go, too. Bye!
Jenny:	Bye!

(Brad and Orlando leave)

Gabby:	I really am sorry, Jenny.
Jenny:	Well, just don't gossip so much next time.
Gabby:	I won't!
Jenny:	Especially if you see me at the theater with another boy.
Gabby:	What?
Jenny:	Yeah – Paul invited me on a date Friday night! But don't tell Brad, OK? I told him I had a lot of homework.
Gabby:	OK. I won't say anything. You're going out with Paul? Oh, I heard some things about Paul! Let me tell you what he did to his LAST girlfriend!
Jenny:	What? What did he do? Tell me!

(Jenny and Gabby leave)

The Bad Tattoo

CAST:

Tattooed girl: Alice
Friends: Kelly
                Curtis
                Amy
New boy: Dylan

SETTING: The school lunchroom.

(Kelly is sitting at a table. Alice joins her.)

Kelly: Alice, what's wrong?

Alice: My life is over. I just want to die.

Kelly: What is it? What happened?

Alice: It's Dylan. He broke up with me this morning!

Kelly: He did? Wow. You two have been going out for only a couple of weeks.

Alice: Twelve days. He found someone he likes better!

Kelly: Wow. I can't believe it.

(Curtis and Amy come over.)

Curtis: What can't you believe?

Kelly: Dylan dumped Alice.

Curtis: He did? *(Smiles)*

Amy: Oh, I'm sorry. But, you know, you might feel bad now, Alice, but it's a good thing. Dylan is stupid. It's good you are not going out with him anymore.

Alice: But he is so cute!

Kelly: Well, yeah. He is cute.

Curtis: That's not helping, Kelly. And he's not that cute.

Kelly: No, I mean – he is cute, but he is not a good guy. You're lucky he's not your boyfriend.

Alice: You don't understand. Last night I got a tattoo!

Amy: You did?

Kelly: What is it? A butterfly or something?

Curtis: Where is it? On your arm or leg?

Alice: The tattoo is Dylan's name. It's "Dylan" with a heart around it. *(She shows them the tattoo.)*

Curtis: His name?

Kelly: Oh, no. But it's not so bad, is it? You can keep it. It will help you remember the good times you had with him.

Alice: It will make me remember how he dumped me!

Amy: Maybe the tattoo people can change it somehow. Make a new word or something.

Alice: A new word? What new word can you make with "Dylan"?

Amy: Well, there's that singer, Bob Dylan. You can put "Bob" on top of "Dylan."

Alice:	I never even heard his music. What if I hate it? I have to tell everyone I love Bob Dylan for the rest of my life?
Curtis:	I think they can cut it out or erase it or something. I think they use lasers.
Alice:	Does it hurt?
Kelly:	Yeah, probably. It probably hurts a lot.
Alice:	Oh! What can I do?
Amy:	Eat your lunch. Class is going to start soon.
Alice:	I'm not hungry. What am I going to do?
Curtis:	Find another boyfriend. There are lots of nice guys around. You can find someone nice. Someone like me, for example. That's just an example.
Amy:	If you like cute guys, look over there.
Alice:	Where?
Amy:	There. The new boy in school. I don't know his name yet, but wow, he is really cute.
Curtis:	Oh, he's not that cute.
Kelly:	No, he really is. But that doesn't fix Alice's problem.
Amy:	What problem? You broke up with Dylan. OK, that's sad. His name is tattooed on you. That's too bad. But find a new boyfriend and forget about Dylan.
Kelly:	And make sure you wear long-sleeved shirts all the time. There. Problem solved!
Alice:	I don't know if I'm ready for a new boyfriend. He'll probably lie to me, just like Dylan did.

Curtis: Not every guy lies. Me, for example. I will never lie to you. I mean, that's just an example.

Alice: I'm talking about boyfriends, Curtis. Not you.

Curtis: Oh. Yeah. I know. It was just an example.

Amy: You've got to forget Dylan. Go say "hi!" to the new boy.

Alice: That doesn't fix my problem. I have a tattoo of "Dylan"!

Curtis: I can lend you some money, so you can get them to cut it out with lasers. Then you can start over with a new guy. Someone like me, maybe. But that's just an example.

Alice: But it would hurt!

Kelly: Yeah. It really would.

Amy: Hey – the new boy is coming this way!

(Dylan enters.)

Amy: Hi!

Dylan: Oh, hi.

Amy: Do you know my friend, here? Her name is Alice.

Dylan: Hi, Alice. Your eyes are red. Are you all right?

Curtis: She's fine. You can go.

Kelly: She had some bad news.

Dylan: Oh, that's too bad. Can I help you somehow?

Amy: Wow, that's really sweet!

Curtis: It's not that sweet. I already said I could help her.

Alice: That is sweet. You're really nice.

Dylan: Oh, I'm glad you think so! I kept looking over here, because… well, because you're so cute.

Alice: Do you think so?

Dylan: Yeah.

Alice: What's your name?

Dylan: I'm Dylan.

Curtis: Dylan? That's the same name as—

Kelly: Shut up, Curtis.

Alice: Dylan. That's a nice name.

Dylan: I'm glad you like it.

Alice: Hey, Dylan. You can sit next to me if you want.

(Dylan sits next to Alice. Curtis gets up and begins to exit.)

Curtis: I have to change my name. That's what I have to do. I have to change my name.

First Week

CAST:

Student: Allan
Advisor
Friends: Danny
            Laurie

SETTING: An advisor's office, then in front of a campus building

MONDAY

(Allan and the Advisor are sitting at a table.)

Advisor: So – do you understand, now? Do you know which classes you have?

Allan: I'm still not sure. I have English 120 in Building 100, Room 330, at 9:15, right? And then Math 210 in Building 101 at 3:15, in Room 101?

Advisor: No, no. Listen again. You have English 100 in Room 330 in Building 915 at 1:20 on Mondays, Wednesdays, and Fridays, then Math 101 in Building 315 in Room 120 at 2:10 on Tuesdays and Thursdays. And then your History 200 class is at 3:50 in Room 305 in Building 104 on Mondays and Thursdays.

Allan: So I have Math, History, and then English?

Advisor: No, you have Math, English, and then History. But not every day.

Allan: Not every day? So that means I don't have class every day?

Advisor: You have class every day, but not the same class. On Mondays you have English and History, and on Tuesdays you have Math, and on Wednesdays you have English, and on Thursdays you have Math and History, and on Fridays you have English.

Allan: Um, OK. I don't really understand. Before I had the same classes every day.

Advisor: Yes, things are different in a university. Don't get confused! You might think you have History on Monday in Room 104, instead of Math on Wednesdays in Room 330.

Allan: That's a lot to remember.

Advisor: All of the information is on your phone. If you forget, just check the app.

Allan: Oh, OK! That's good.

Advisor: So – are you ready for your first day in academic class? Are you excited?

Allan: Yeah. A little nervous, too.

Advisor: That's normal. You will be fine. Come back and see me if you have any problems.

Allan: OK. Thanks!

Advisor: Good luck.

(Advisor leaves.)

(Allan walks out and sees his friend, Danny.)

Allan: Hey, Danny!

Danny: Hi!

Allan: You look unhappy. What's wrong?

Danny: I had my first academic class today.

Allan: How was it?

Danny: Oh, terrible! I couldn't understand the teacher at all! He spoke so fast, and he used a lot of strange words.

Allan: I'm sure you will be fine. You just need a little time.

Danny: Have you had your first class yet?

Allan: No, I need to find it now. Let me check my phone.

Danny: Hey, there's Laurie.

Allan: Laurie? Really? Hey – hey, Laurie!

(Laurie arrives.)

Laurie: Hi, guys.

Danny: Hi.

Allan: Hey, Laurie! How are you doing?

Laurie: Fine. How about you?

Allan: Fine!

Danny: He's worried about his first academic class.

Allan: No, no. I'm not worried. No problem.

Danny: He doesn't even remember what room it's in. He has to check his phone.

Laurie: Well, it can be confusing.

Allan: Confusing? Well, maybe for some people, I guess. I have a great memory.

Laurie:	Really? You can remember all the buildings and room numbers and times?
Allan:	Sure! I don't need to check my phone.
Laurie:	Wow.
Danny:	Really? You don't need to check?
Allan:	No, I remember. No problem. I have a great memory.
Danny:	So where is your first class, then?
Allan:	Um, right here. I have English 100 in Room 120 in Building 330.
Laurie:	Wow, you can remember all that on your first day?
Allan:	Sure.
Laurie:	You should probably check your schedule, just to make sure.
Allan:	No, I'm fine. Like I said, I've got a great memory.
Laurie:	Well, I've got to go. I have a Psychology class in five minutes.
Allan:	Hey, let's go out for dinner this Friday, and celebrate our first week in academic classes.
Laurie:	Great. I'll meet you here on Friday.
Danny:	Yeah, I can make it.
Allan:	Oh – you're coming, too? OK, I guess.
	(Laurie leaves.)
Danny:	Bye!
Allan:	Bye, Laurie! Maybe I'll see you after class? Laurie?
	(Allan starts to follow Laurie as if hypnotized, but Danny pulls him back.)

Danny: She's already gone, Allan.

Allan: She sure is nice.

Danny: You have class now, too, right?

Allan: Oh, yeah! I have to hurry. See you!

(Allan and Danny exit, in different directions.)

FRIDAY

(Allan is alone. Danny enters.)

Danny: Hey, Allan! How's it going?

Allan: Oh, hey. Fine, I guess.

Danny: You don't look fine. Something wrong?

Allan: I guess I'm just tired.

Danny: It's been a long first week, hasn't it?

Allan: You think so, too? I feel like a stupid person. I can't understand anything in my class!

(Laurie enters)

Laurie: Hi, guys!

Allan: Hi. How was your first week?

Laurie: Great. I think I'm really going to enjoy all my classes.

Allan: They're not too hard?

Laurie: Well, they're not easy. At first it was hard to understand the professor. But I think it's going to be fine.

Danny: Allan has had a hard time.

Laurie:	Oh, really? I'm sorry to hear that.
Allan:	I feel so stupid! I just don't understand anything!
Laurie:	Oh, come on. You understand SOME things, right?
Allan:	No, nothing!
Laurie:	How about at the beginning of class? Doesn't the professor say "Good morning" or something? You can understand that!
Allan:	I don't understand a thing he says! Not one thing!
Danny:	Wow. Who's your professor, anyway?
Allan:	I only know THAT because he wrote his name on the board the first day. Professor Mumpower.
Danny:	Hmmm. I wonder if he is famous for being hard. Let me look him up on the Internet.
Laurie:	A professor you can't understand – wow. I can't believe the college even gave him a job.
Allan:	Yeah. He's really bad.
Danny:	Um, Allan?
Allan:	Yeah?
Danny:	Where's your classroom, again?
Allan:	Room 120 in Building 330.
Danny:	Something is strange. Let me look up your class schedule.
Laurie:	What is it?
Danny:	Yeah – I found the problem.
Allan:	What problem?

Danny: Room 120 in Building 330 is Advanced German, not English 100.

Allan: What?

Danny: Yeah. See? You were supposed to go to English 100 in Building 915. You were in the wrong class all this time!

Laurie: Advanced German – no wonder you couldn't understand anything! Your professor wasn't even speaking English!

Allan: I can't believe it.

Danny: You thought you had such a perfect memory!

Allan: Oh, come on. Anyone could make a mistake like that. Let's go have dinner.

Laurie: No, I think we'd better go make an appointment for you to talk to your advisor, first!

(Laurie pulls Allan offstage, and Danny exits also.)

Can I Pass?

CAST:

Teacher: Ms. Taylor
Colleague: Ms. Colly
Student: Wilson
Other Students

SETTING: Teacher's Office

Taylor: Oh, I am so glad that this quarter is almost over!

Colly: Yes, me too. I am so tired.

Taylor: Are you almost finished?

Colly: Well, I have to grade these final essays, and then put the grades into the computer, but after that I am done.

Taylor: I just have to finish grading the final exams. Did you have a good class this quarter?

Colly: Pretty good. I had some great students. They didn't sleep in class. They paid attention. They did their homework. They asked good questions. They studied before the tests.

Taylor: They sound great!

Colly: Yes. Of course, I did have some lazy students, also.

Taylor: Me, too. But most of my students were really good. I will miss them when they leave. You know, I am tired, but I still really love my job!

Colly: Me, too. But right now, I have to go to the restroom!

(She leaves.)

(There is a knock at the door. Taylor opens it.)

Taylor: Wilson! Hi! Do you need something?

Wilson: Hi, Ms. Taylor. Can I talk to you?

Taylor: Well, OK. Come in. Sit down. What is it?

Wilson: I'm worried about my grade.

Taylor: Yes. I understand. Your grades were not too good this quarter.

Wilson: Can I still pass?

Taylor: I don't think it's possible, but let's look at your grades. Hmmm. You missed six homework assignments, your midterm exam was 43%, and you copied your essay from the Internet. Also, you didn't get a grade for your research project.

Wilson: But I did it! I gave it to you.

Taylor: It was three weeks late. Remember, the rule is that if it's that late, I don't grade it.

Wilson: So if you grade it now, I can pass?

Taylor: No, I can't grade it. It was handed in too late.

Wilson: So, you don't think I can pass?

Taylor: No, your grades are not good enough. Sorry.

Wilson: But I really want to pass.

Taylor: I'm sorry. You have to do the work if you want to pass. You haven't done the work.

Wilson: But my parents will be very upset if I don't pass.

Taylor: Well, maybe you can tell your parents that you will work hard next quarter. And then you really DO have to work hard next quarter.

Wilson: I don't think my parents will believe me.

Taylor: I don't think I would, either.

Wilson: Can I make up the missing homework assignments?

Taylor: No, sorry. It's too late.

Wilson: So what can I do? I really want to pass.

Taylor: There's nothing you can do, now. It's too late. The quarter is over.

Wilson: So how can I pass?

Taylor: You can't.

Wilson: Do you have any extra credit assignments I can do?

Taylor: If I give you extra credit, it wouldn't be fair to the other students. And anyway, it's too late now.

Wilson: But then I can't pass.

Taylor: No, you can't.

Wilson: Oh.

(There is a long pause.)

Really?

Taylor: Yes, really. I'm sorry.

Wilson: Can you help me pass?

Taylor: I tried to help you all quarter. I told you that you could go to the Writing Center for help. Did you go?

Wilson: I was busy.

Taylor:	I told you that you could ask for help with your research project at the library. Did you do that?
Wilson:	No, I didn't.
Taylor:	I told you that I would help anyone with their homework, or answer any questions, if you came to talk to me in my office. Did you come?
Wilson:	No, I didn't. But I am here now.
Taylor:	Now the quarter is over. It's too late.
Wilson:	But maybe I can—
Taylor:	It's too late.
Wilson:	How about if I—
Taylor:	It's too late.
Wilson:	If I handed in all my—
Taylor:	It's too late.
Wilson:	It's too late?
Taylor:	That's right. It's too late.
Wilson:	So what can I do?
Taylor:	There's nothing you can do now. It's too late.
Wilson:	OK. I guess it's too late.
Taylor:	That's right.
Wilson:	OK.
Taylor:	I hope you will try harder next quarter. The teachers and advisors are all here to help you, but you need to do your work yourself. OK?
Wilson:	So if I promise that NEXT quarter I will work hard, will you let me

	pass this quarter?
Taylor:	No.
Wilson:	OK.
Taylor:	OK, then. Goodbye.
Wilson:	Bye.

(Wilson walks away, to join several other students. Taylor stays at her desk, her head in her hands.)

Taylor:	Aarrghh!

(Colly comes back into the office.)

Colly:	Hey – are you all right?
Taylor:	I just had a student in here. He didn't work all quarter – didn't do his homework, cheated on the tests, came late to class, copied his essays from the Internet. And now he comes in here begging to pass!
Colly:	Oh, I hate that! Did he keep saying "Can you help me pass?"
Taylor:	Exactly! It makes me crazy!
Colly:	I know how you feel! But think about this. You only had one student come to complain to you. Now you can relax.
Taylor:	Yes, that's true. It was just one student. One quarter I had three people, all asking me to help them pass!
Colly:	Yeah. It was just one. You're lucky.
Taylor:	I guess you're right.
Colly:	Well, I'm going home now. Have a good break!
Taylor:	Yeah, you too! Bye.

(Colly leaves.)

Taylor: Yeah, it was just one student. I'll be OK. One student won't make me crazy.

(Outside the office, Wilson is talking to several other students. Taylor doesn't know they are there, and doesn't hear them.)

Wilson: Well, I did the best I could, but she wouldn't let me pass. Maybe I gave up too soon. I should have talked to her longer. Well, I hope you have better luck than I did!

Student 1: OK. But now I want to talk to her! I really want to pass!

Student 3: No – I want to talk to her! I want to pass!

Student 2: No! It's my turn! I'm next! I need to pass!

(Wilson leaves. Student knocks on the door.)

Student 2: Hi, Ms. Taylor. Can I talk to you?

Taylor: *(Hides behind desk, whimpering.)* No – no, no!

The Diamond Job

CAST:

DB
Cassidy
Jessie
Billy

SETTING: A street outside a jewelry store, at night

> (DB is standing on the street, looking around nervously. Cassidy and Jessie enter.)

DB: There you guys are! Where have you been? You're late!

Cassidy: We're not late. It's 12:30, just like we planned.

DB: OK, OK. But where's Billy? He should be here.

Cassidy: He'll probably be here soon. Just wait.

Jessie: I don't like that he's late. I wonder about him.

DB: What do you mean?

Jessie: I mean I don't know him very well. He might be… you know.

DB: What?

Jessie: You know. He might be with the police.

DB: A cop? Do you think so?

Jessie:	Yeah. Sometimes the police pretend to be bad guys, so they can catch us.
DB:	I can't believe it! I'll kill him!
Cassidy:	Now, relax. We don't know he's a cop.
DB:	If he's a cop, we're dead! We're all dead!
Cassidy:	We don't know he's a cop. Take it easy.
Jessie:	I don't trust him. I think he's a cop. When we take the diamonds, he'll arrest all of us!
DB:	Do you think so? Maybe we shouldn't steal the diamonds!
Cassidy:	We don't know he's a cop! Let's steal the diamonds. We will all be rich!
DB:	We'll all be in jail if Billy is a cop.
Jessie:	Look! Here comes Billy!

(Billy enters)

Billy:	Hi, guys. Is everyone ready?
DB:	I don't know.
Billy:	What do you mean? We planned to steal the diamonds tonight.
Jessie:	Before we steal any diamonds, we have to be sure.
Billy:	Sure about what?
Cassidy:	DB and Jessie think you might be a police officer, Billy.
Billy:	Me, a police officer? Ha! That's crazy!
Cassidy:	See? I told you.
DB:	How can we be sure that you are telling the truth?

Billy: Come on, guys! We're been planning on stealing these diamonds for months! We have worked together for a long time!

Jessie: You might be a cop. We can't trust you.

Billy: Oh, yeah? Well, maybe it's not me. Maybe someone else is a cop.

Cassidy: What? Who? Who's the cop?

Billy: Jessie says I'm a cop. Maybe that is because he is trying to hide something.

Jessie: Like what? I don't have any secrets! What do you think I'm hiding?

Billy: You want everyone to think I am a cop because really YOU are a cop!

(Billy pulls a gun and points it at Jessie.) Maybe I can't trust YOU!

Jessie: *(Jessie pulls a gun and points it at Billy.)* I'm not a cop!

Cassidy: Guys, guys! Relax! Just put the guns away!

Billy: Why do you want us to put the guns away, Cassidy?

DB: Yeah – why? Maybe YOU'RE a cop! *(DB pulls a gun and points it at Cassidy.)* Don't move!

Cassidy: Hey – what's that? *(Cassidy points off to the side. Everyone looks, and Cassidy draws his gun.)* YOU don't move, DB! Maybe YOU are the cop!

Jessie: Wait – so who's the cop?

DB: Cassidy!

Jessie: I thought Billy was the cop.

Billy: No, YOU'RE the cop!

Cassidy: Guys, come on! DB is the cop!

DB: No I'm not! It's you – or Billy. Maybe Jessie. I don't know!

Jessie: Well, SOMEONE is the cop!

Billy: But who?

Cassidy: I thought it was DB, but now I'm not sure.

DB: I thought it was Jessie. But maybe it's DB. Or Cassidy. I'm not sure anymore!

Billy: Maybe we should all quietly put our guns down, and try to figure this out.

Jessie: Maybe you want us to put our guns down because you're the cop!

DB: Yeah. You put your gun down first, Billy.

Billy: I'm not going to do it first! You'll shoot me!

Cassidy: No wants to put their gun down first. So – what do we do?

Jessie: I don't know.

DB: Well, we have to figure out who is the cop.

Billy: Yeah – we have to know who is the cop.

Jessie: It's not me.

Cassidy: I'm not a cop.

Billy: It's not me! At least, I don't think so. DB:

You're not sure if you are a cop or not?

Billy: I thought I was sure, but now I am confused.

DB: Yeah, me too. Maybe I'm the cop. I just don't know!

Jessie: Maybe all of us are cops. Is that possible?

Cassidy:	I guess so. I don't know.
DB:	None of us knows.
Billy:	So what do we do? Do we still rob the store and get the diamonds?
Jessie:	If we do that, and if we are all cops, we'll all go to jail.
DB:	You're right.
Cassidy:	Maybe we should just go home.
Jessie:	I think you're right.
Billy:	So we don't get the diamonds? We don't get rich?
Cassidy:	I guess not.

(Everyone puts their guns away.)

DB:	I'll never get rich. Cops don't make much money, you know.
Jessie:	Yeah, it's terrible. My wife always complains about that.
Billy:	They should pay us more. We do a dangerous job.
Cassidy:	You're right. We almost got killed tonight! But no one cares, I guess.
DB:	Well, let's not think about it. See you at work tomorrow, guys.
Billy:	Yeah. See you.
Jessie:	Bye.
Cassidy:	See you guys tomorrow.

(Everyone exits.)

Detectives

CAST:

Detectives: Renko
            Lucy
Killer: Mick Belker

SETTING: Anywhere

(A dead body is on the ground. Over it stands Mick, a bloody knife in his hands.)

(Renko and Lucy arrive.)

Lucy: *(Raising gun)* Police! Freeze!

Renko: Oh, put the gun down, Lucy.

Lucy: But—

Renko: We don't point guns at witnesses! What were you thinking? *(To Mick)* How are you, sir? Did you see what happened here?

Mick: Uh, I'm not sure.

Renko: Let's look at the body, Lucy. Hmm. I see some big cuts.

Lucy: Of course, detective Renko! Cuts from that knife!

Renko: Now, now, Lucy. We don't know that. A person can be cut in many different ways. Maybe he was cutting vegetables, and accidentally cut himself.

Lucy: But he's not in a kitchen! And there is no knife in his hands!

Renko:	Good point. Maybe he wasn't cutting vegetables. Maybe we should ask this witness some questions. What is your name, sir?
Mick:	My name? I'm Mick. Mick Belker.
Renko:	Do you know this man?
Mick:	Of course I knew him! He was sleeping with my wife!
Renko:	He was?
Mick:	Sure he was! And so I – I mean, no. I don't know him.
Lucy:	You just told us he was sleeping with your wife.
Mick:	I probably made a mistake. Maybe it was another guy.
Renko:	I understand, sir. Just relax. It's easy to get confused. What did you see? Did you see this man die?
Mick:	I work at night, and I found him in my home this morning. I caught him with my wife! He ran out of my house. So I chased him here, and I took my knife, raised it over my head…
Lucy:	Yes? Then what?
Mick:	I, um, I don't remember. I think he just had a heart attack or something. Maybe he was sick.
Lucy:	Sick? That's crazy! Look at him! Look at all the blood!
Renko:	Calm down, Lucy. Are you a doctor?
Lucy:	No, I'm a police detective.
Renko:	And I am not a doctor, either. We don't know if he was sick or not. Maybe some kinds of sickness cause big cuts in the body.
Lucy:	Why don't you ask Belker why there is so much blood on the knife in his hands?

Renko:	OK, I guess we can do that. Well, sir? Why is there so much blood on your knife?
Mick:	Blood? Oh, I – yeah, I know. I was cutting some chicken for dinner.
Renko:	OK. See, Lucy? He has a good answer.
Lucy:	It's nine o'clock in the morning.
Renko:	Yes, it is.
Lucy:	Well, who cooks dinner at nine o'clock in the morning?
Renko:	Mr. Belker, here, does that, Lucy. He just told us.
Lucy:	Ohhh!
Renko:	This is a very mysterious case.
Lucy:	No, it's really not!
Renko:	There's no way to know what happened here.
Lucy:	There really is!
Renko:	We don't even know the victim's name. Can you find any ID on him?
Mick:	His name was Furillo. Frank Furillo.
Lucy:	So you do know him!
Mick:	No – I, I um, I just guessed.
Renko:	Look – here is his ID. Frank Furillo. Thank you, sir. That was a good guess.
Mick:	Yeah. Uh, can I go now?
Lucy:	Now, wait a minute! He has a bloody knife in his hands. He says the man was sleeping with his wife. He knew the man's name!
Renko:	What are you trying to say, Lucy?

Lucy:	That the man is guilty! He's the killer! Come on! It's so easy to see!
Renko:	Hmm. I see what you mean. Maybe he really is a bad guy.
Lucy:	Finally!
Renko:	Yes. Look at this. *(Renko picks a candy wrapper from the ground.)*
Lucy:	It's garbage. Just a candy wrapper.
Renko:	Yes, that's right! Sir, you are under arrest! *(Renko handcuffs Mick)*
Lucy:	Yes – for murder!
Renko:	Murder? No, no – for littering! He must have thrown this garbage on the ground! Next time, sir, find a garbage can!
Lucy:	I don't believe this.
Renko:	Believe it, Lucy. This city is full of terrible people. Take him to the police station!
Lucy:	Um, sir? When I get there, can I check the blood on the knife for DNA?
Renko:	Well, I guess that's OK. I don't understand why, but fine. Let's go.
Lucy:	What about the dead man?
Renko:	He's not going anywhere.

(Renko, Lucy, and Mick exit.)

The Ghosts

CAST:

New ghost: Pinky
Scary Ghosts: Boo
          Hiss
Mother: Mom
Child: Kyra

SETTING: a living room

(Mom and Kyra are looking at their phones, eating popcorn. Boo and Hiss are nearby, but unseen by the living.)

Boo: Whooo! Whoaahh!

Hiss: I like it! Sounds good! Let me try. Eeeewwwooh! Eeeaaahh!

Boo: Yeah, that's good. It's really scary.

Hiss: Good! Let's scare this family! A mother and a child, alone in the night. This will be great.

Boo: No, no, wait. A new ghost is joining us tonight.

Hiss: A new ghost?

Boo: Yeah. Her name is… (*consults a paper*) Pinky. Yeah, Pinky. She just died a few days ago. This is her first time to be a ghost, so we have to teach her.

Hiss: Why do we have to teach her?

Boo: Maybe because we are the scariest ghosts in town.

Hiss: Yeah, that makes sense. We can show her how to be a very scary ghost.

(Pinky arrives)

Boo: Here she comes now. Hi!

Pinky: Hi. I'm Pinky.

Boo: I'm Boo, and this is Hiss. Are you ready to learn how to be a scary ghost?

Pinky: I guess so. I don't know much about how to be a ghost.

Hiss: That's all right. We'll show you. It's not hard.

Boo: Right. Before you came in, we were practicing our scary noises. Here is mine: Whooo! Whoaahh!

Pinky: Wow! You're good.

Hiss: My scary sound is Eeeewwwooh! Eeeaaahh!

Pinky: That's really good, too.

Boo: Thanks! Now you try. Make a scary noise!

Pinky: I don't know any scary noises.

Boo: Just make a sound.

Pinky: Well, OK. Here I go. Ahem. Teedalee! Teedaleedalee!

(Pause)

How was that?

Hiss: Well, it was OK… but it wasn't really too scary.

Boo: No, it was a happy sound. A scary sound can be something like Aaahhhh! or Oooooaaah!

The Playbook

Hiss: Or Eeeeeoooo! Or maybe Bwahahaha!

Pinky: OK. I see. Let me try again.

Boo: Go ahead.

Pinky: All right. Here I go. Falalala! Falalalalala! Was that better?

Boo: Not really.

Hiss: It might even be worse. But listen – you don't really have to make scary noises to be a scary ghost.

Pinky: I don't?

Hiss: No. You can do other things. For example, we can make scary walking sounds. Like this. *(Makes loud, slow stomping sounds.)*

Boo: Or like this. *(Drags one foot and walks loudly.)* **Now you try.**

Pinky: OK. How about this? *(Does a cheerful tap dance.)*

Hiss: Oh, no, no.

Boo: Maybe scary walking sounds is not your thing.

Pinky: But what else can I try? Hey – I heard that ghosts can affect electricity. Is that right? We can turn lights on and off, turn the radio on and off, and stuff like that.

Boo: Yes, we can do that. But it's not really too scary. People just think the power is out.

Pinky: Then what should I do?

Hiss: I know. You can make things float in the air.

Pinky: How do I do that?

Hiss: Well, see the mother and daughter there?

Pinky: Sure.

Hiss:	Well, they can't see you. So if you pick something up, and walk around with it, it will look like it is floating in the air!
Pinky:	Oh, that sounds like fun! Let me try!
	(Pinky walks over to Mom and Kyra and picks up a magazine. She flies the magazine in front of the people, but Kyra and Mom are too interested in her phones. Pinky comes back to the other ghosts.)
	It doesn't work! They didn't even notice!
Boo:	Yeah, I don't get it. They never even looked up.
Pinky:	They just look at their phones.
Hiss:	Their phones? Is that what those things are? They're phones?
Pinky:	Sure. Don't you know about cellphones? Everyone has them nowadays.
Boo:	I died fifty years ago.
Hiss:	And I died almost a hundred years ago. No one had those things.
Boo:	And now they look at them all the time. They don't even look up, so how can you scare them? It's a problem.
Hiss:	I don't know what to do!
Pinky:	Maybe I am just not scary. I am a terrible ghost! *(Pinky cries.)*
Boo:	Oh, it will be all right.
Hiss:	Yeah. Hey -- maybe we should take a little break.
Pinky:	Good idea. *(Pinky regains control of herself and glances at the mother and daughter.)* Hey, the mom is watching a movie on her phone. That might cheer me up. Let's go check it out.

Boo: She can watch a movie on her phone? I want to see this!

Hiss: Yeah. It might be fun.

(Boo, Hiss, and Pinky gather around the phone. Suddenly they all laugh, as does Mom.)

Boo: That was funny!

Hiss: Yeah! I like this new technology!

(They continue to watch. They all laugh again.)

Mom: OK, Kyra. Time for bed.

Kyra: Oh, I don't want to go to bed! I'm playing with my phone!

Mom: You can play with it in the morning. Time for bed!

Kyra: Oh, all right.

(Mom and Kyra plug in their phones and leave.)

Hiss: They went to bed. Now maybe they will hear our scary sounds.

Boo: Right. But Pinky can't make any scary sounds.

Pinky: Guys, I think I have an idea.

Hiss: You do?

Boo: What is it?

Pinky: We can control electricity, right?

Boo: Right. It's not scary, though.

Pinky: You'll see.

THE NEXT MORNING

>*(Mom and Kyra rush to their phones.)*

Mom: Good morning. *(She picks up her phone.)*

Kyra: Good morning. *(She picks up her phone.)*

Mom: What the...?

Pinky: Now – look what happens!

Kyra: Mom – Mom! My phone is dead! I can't text my friends! I can't check my Instagram!

Boo: You stopped the electricity in their phones. They hate it!

Mom: My phone is dead, too! Dead! Dead! No Facebook – no Internet!

Hiss: Look how scared they are!

Boo: Congratulations, Pinky! You did it! You found a way to scare them!

Kyra: No phone? No Internet? No texting? No...no! Ahhhhhhhhhh! Ahhhhhhhh!

Mom: Ahhhhhhhh! Ahhhhh! Ahhhhhhhhh!

Cleaning Up

CAST:
John
Paul
George

SETTING: A messy apartment

(Paul and George are sitting in the living room. George is reading a book and Paul is looking at a magazine. John enters.)

John: Guys, we have a problem with the toilet.

George: Again? What happened?

John: Well, you know. It's clogged. It won't flush.

Paul: You broke it. You always break the toilet. What do you eat?

John: It's not my fault. It's just not a good toilet.

(John picks up a bag of potato chips.)

George: Did you try to fix it?

John: No. I don't know how to fix a toilet.

Paul: Well, I'm not going to do it!

George: Ahhrggh! (*Leaves room.*)

John: It's just not a good toilet.

Paul: Yeah. Blame the toilet.

John: Hey, I'm hungry. What's for dinner tonight?

Paul: I don't know. Maybe I have enough money for pizza. *(Looks in wallet.)* Nope. Hey, is there any pizza left in that box?

John: No, we ate the last piece two weeks ago. Isn't there anything in the refrigerator?

Paul: Not much. Just a couple of tomatoes and onions.

(George comes back in the room, his sleeves wet, wiping his hands on a towel.)

George: OK. The toilet is fixed.

Paul: Great. Hey, what's for dinner?

George: I don't know.

Paul: Didn't you make anything?

George: No. Did you?

Paul: Come on, everyone knows I am a terrible cook.

John: Me, too. I can't cook at all. But you're a good cook, George.

Paul: Yeah. You're good.

George: Well, I don't know what to cook. I think we have a little hamburger meat.

John: Paul said there were onions and tomatoes in the refrigerator.

George: OK. So, I can I can fry them up with the hamburger and some potatoes.

(Paul throws his magazine on the floor.)

Paul: Let's go to a movie or something. I'm bored.

George: If you're bored, maybe you could spend a little time cleaning up the apartment. Like that magazine you just threw on the floor.

Paul: What about it? I'm finished with it.

George: So put it in the recycling.

John: Ha! I've never seen Paul clean anything up! *(He picks up a bag of potato chips and starts eating them.)*

George: You don't clean up, either.

John: I'm just not good at cleaning.

Paul: Yeah. That's your job, George.

George: I dream about the day I have enough money to get my own apartment! Why is everything my job?

John: Not everything.

Paul: Yeah. Just cleaning, cooking, washing dishes, that kind of thing.

George: I'm tired of doing all the work in this apartment. I don't understand why you two can't help.

John: I would like to help, but I'm just not good at it.

George: Then what are you good at?

Paul: Sleeping!

John: Yeah. And playing on my phone!

George: I don't know why I stay here with you guys!

Paul: It's because we pay half of the rent!

George: That's not fair. I pay half, and you two pay half?

Paul: That's what we agreed to!

George: Well, it's not fair. I think you should pay more in rent.

Paul: I don't have any extra money!

George: Well, you've got to give me something! This really isn't fair.

Paul: OK, OK – um, here's some candy I found in my pocket. It's yours.

George: Candy?

Paul: It's better than nothing. *(Paul stuffs candy in George's hand.)*

George: I can't believe this! It's old and sticky! And how about you, John?

John: Have some potato chips.

George: I don't want any potato chips!

John: OK. Let me see what I've got in my pockets. No candy. Oh, here – have a lottery ticket. I bought ten of them.

George: You bought ten lottery tickets? I told you we needed to buy some toilet paper, and you said you didn't have any money! How did you find the money to buy lottery tickets?

John: I don't know. I guess I found some extra money. Take the ticket.

(John gives George a lottery ticket.)

There. Feel better, now? I don't want to hear any more complain- ing about housework. Paul gave you candy. I gave you a ticket that could mean a lot of money. End of conversation.

Paul: You gave him a lottery ticket? He could win hundreds of dollars!

John:	I gave him one lottery ticket. I have ten! He won't win anything! I play it all the time. I never win anything.
	(George scratches his ticket.)
George:	Hmmm. It looks like – yes! Amazing! Yes – I just won ten million dollars!
John:	What?
Paul:	No way!
George:	Yes, I did! See the numbers? I won ten million dollars!
John:	Give that back to me!
George:	But you gave it to me.
John:	Maybe we could share. Can't we talk about it?
George:	"End of conversation" is what you said, right?
Paul:	Ha! You're right, George! That's what he said! Oh, man, we're going to have good times, now! George can get us a new TV, and new phones, and a better apartment, and…
	(George puts on his jacket.)
	Hey, George! What are you doing?
George:	I'm going to get my money.
John:	And then after you come back we can talk about—
George:	I'm not coming back.
Paul:	Oh, come on, George!
George:	No, I'm not coming back. You two can worry about paying the rent. You can unclog the toilet. You can make dinner.

(George takes the bag of potato chips from John and scatters them on the floor.)

And you can clean up!

(George exits.)

Paul: Give me some chips. *(Starts eating chips from the floor)*

John: Hey! Those are mine! *(Fights Paul over chips.)*

The Cheaters

CAST:
Cheaters: Chip
            Darlene
Student: Evan
Teacher: Ms. Forsythe
Other Students

SETTING: A classroom

Chip: Hey, Darlene!

Darlene: Hey. So you found our new classroom.

Chip: Yeah. I guess our regular classroom has a broken window.

Darlene: I wonder who broke the window!

Chip: Yeah, how did that happen? I have no idea!

            (They both laugh.)

Chip: Are you ready for this test?

Darlene: No! Are you?

Chip: No way. I didn't study all week. I was playing League of Legends with my friends. I am going to bomb this test.

Darlene: I forgot we had a test today. I'm not ready at all. Hey, there's our teacher. *(To Forsythe)* Um, Ms. Forsythe? Ms. Forsythe, I have a question?

Forsythe:	Yes, Darlene? What is it?
Darlene:	Well, I forgot we had a test today, so I didn't study.
Forsythe:	You forgot? I talked about the test every day this week.
Darlene:	I guess I didn't hear you.
Forsythe:	I also wrote "Test Friday!" on the board.
Darlene:	I guess I didn't see it.
Forsythe:	And yesterday I gave you notes about what is going to be on the test.
Darlene:	I guess I didn't read it.
Forsythe:	Well, I can't help you.
Darlene:	Maybe we could have the test on Monday? I promise I will study!
Forsythe:	I'm sorry, Darlene, but everyone else studied. It's not fair to change the time now.
Darlene:	But I'm not ready!
Forsythe:	You should have paid attention.
	(Forsythe leaves)
Darlene:	She is so unfair!
Chip:	She's not just unfair. She's mean! How can she do this to us?
Darlene:	What are we going to do? If I fail this test, my mom will kill me.
Chip:	Yeah, and my parents said if I fail one more test I have to go to extra classes in the summer. It's so unfair!
Darlene:	Hey, who is that?
Chip:	I don't recognize him. But look! He has all those notes.

Darlene:	I bet he studied for this stupid test.
Chip:	Yeah. He probably studied ten hours a day. No way is he going to fail.
Darlene:	He'll probably get an A-Plus. It's so unfair.
Chip:	Really unfair.
Darlene:	Hey, I got an idea. We can sit next to him. You sit on one side, and I can sit on the other side.
Chip:	Why?
Darlene:	So we can copy his paper!
Chip:	Oh, yeah. Great idea! Let's go before someone else has the same idea.

(Darlene and Chip sit next to Evan.)

Darlene:	Hi. I'm Darlene.
Evan:	Hey. Evan.
Darlene:	Well, nice to meet you, Evan!
Evan:	Yeah, sure.
Forsythe:	OK, everyone. Let's get ready for the test. Put away your phones. You only need a pencil.
Darlene:	Oh, this test is going to be really easy, right?
Evan:	Yeah – I studied all week. Hey, something is strange. Is this room 213?
Darlene:	What are you talking about?
Forsythe:	Quiet, everyone.

(Forysthe passes out the tests.)

(They work on their tests. Darlene can see Evan's test, and copies his answers. Chip can't see it, and become frustrated.)

Chip: Darlene! Darlene!

Forsythe: Quiet, please.

(Darlene drops her pencil under Evan's desk, and looks at him for help. When Evan bends down to get the pencil, Chip copies his test. Evan returns the pencil to Darlene.)

(They work. Soon, Chip becomes frustrated again.)

Chip: Darlene!

Forsythe: Is someone talking over there?

Darlene: *(Holds up three fingers. Pretends to cough.)* Bee-bee ughh ughh. *(Holds up four fingers, and coughs again.)* Eigh-eigh uggh ughh.

Forsythe: Are you feeling all right, Darlene?

Darlene: Ugghh Ughh. Just a little cough, Ms. Forsythe.

Forsythe: One more minute, everybody.

Evan: *(Raises his hand.)* Um, teacher?

Forsythe: Yes, what is it? *(Looks harder at Evan.)* Why – who are you?

Evan: I'm confused. Is this Math class?

Forsythe: No, no. This is History. We had to change rooms. Didn't you see the note on the door? Math class is in room 283 today.

Evan: Oh, no! I guess I'm in the wrong room.

Chip: What?

Forsythe: Well, you'd better get to room 283 as fast as you can.

Evan: Yeah!

(Evan leaves. Chip and Darlene look at each other, dismayed.)

Darlene: Huh?

Forsythe: OK, everyone. Time's up. Please hand in your tests.

(Chip and Darlene hand in their tests.)

Chip: That stupid kid Evan made us fail the test!

Darlene: Yeah. I hate him! He's so mean. He cheated us! It's so unfair. Now we'll be in big trouble.

Chip: I can't believe he did that to us. I'm going to wait for him after school. I'll beat him up!

Darlene: I'll help you! We'll show him what we do to cheaters in this school!

The New Teacher

CAST:

New Teacher: Nellie
Teachers: Steve
            Carla
            Matt

SETTING: A teachers' room

Nellie: Hi, everyone! I'm Nellie. I'm the new teacher.

Steve: Hi, Nellie! Welcome to Red River High School! I'm Steven. That's Carla...

Carla: Humph.

Steve: ...and that's Matt.

Matt: Hey.

Steve: You're going to love it here!

Nellie: I hope so. I'm very nervous! This is the first time I ever had my own class to teach!

Steve: Exciting! Here – you can sit here.

Nellie: Thanks! *(to Carla)* Have you been teaching here long?

Carla: Much too long.

Steve: Ah, Carla likes to joke!

Carla:	It's no joke, believe me.
Nellie:	Wow, I can't believe I am finally a teacher! I don't even know where to start!
Matt:	Well, we have our office supplies over there. Books, pencils, staplers, things like that. That might be a good place to start.
Nellie:	Good idea! I wonder – why do you need a new teacher? What happened to the teacher who had the class before me?
Matt:	Sadly, she died last week.
Nellie:	Oh! She died? Really?
Matt:	Yes. A terrible accident. She fell out of a window.
Nellie:	How sad!
Carla:	Not sad at all. She was the lucky one. She got out of this place. I think the students pushed her out of the window.
Nellie:	Really?
Steve:	No, no, Carla has her jokes. Yes, it was very sad. The old teacher jumped out of a window. But no students were in the room. Terrible. She was a great teacher, and she had a great class. You will love them.
Nellie:	Well, I hope the class likes me.
Steve:	Sure they will!
Matt:	You'll be fine.
Carla:	Humph.
Nellie:	How much homework do you usually give to the students?
Steve:	Not much. I think it's more important to make sure they have fun in class. Keep them active. Keep them thinking.

Nellie: Oh. How about you, Matt?

Matt: I expect them to work an hour or two on homework every night. They're in high school, so they should know how to work hard. I want them to be ready for college.

Nellie: And how about you, Carla?

Carla: Homework? More work for me to grade. I hate it! I have enough problems.

Nellie: You don't give any homework?

Carla: Well, the truth is, I hate grading it, but the kids hate it even more. So I give them lots and lots of homework. If I have to suffer, they should have to suffer, too, right?

Nellie: Oh, I see.

Steve: Here are the textbooks your class is using.

Nellie: Oh, thanks! These look interesting. I bet the students love them.

Carla: The students love drawing pictures in them, and leaving them on the bus, and tearing the pages.

Matt: Not all the students do that, Carla.

Carla: Most of them do. And most of them don't even open their books.

Nellie: But if they don't open their books, how do they pass?

Carla: I don't pass them. I don't want to see them again next year, but if they want to fail, that's fine with me.

Steve: Carla's joking again.

Carla: No, I'm not.

Matt: Some of the students don't use their textbooks much, and they might not pass. But others work hard, and they usually pass.

Steve:	I think it's important to have a good time in class. I usually pass all my students.
Nellie:	Even the ones that don't study?
Steve:	Sure. If they don't understand something, they can learn it next year, right?
Carla:	No, they won't. They don't learn anything.
Matt:	Some do. It just takes a little work.
Carla:	Work! They don't work, and I shouldn't have to work so much, either.
Nellie:	Don't you like teaching, Carla?
Carla:	No, I don't! I really don't.
Nellie:	What would you rather do?
Carla:	Anything! Farm potatoes, clean toilets, drive a truck – anything! I really hate my job! I hate the kids, too!
Nellie:	Wow.
Steve:	There goes Carla and her jokes again!
Matt:	It's almost time for class. Are you ready, Nellie?
Nellie:	I don't know. I thought I was ready. I was really excited! Now – I don't know. I'm not sure if I want to do this or not.
Matt:	You'll be fine.
Steve:	Oh, you'll love it! And the kids will love you, too!
Nellie:	Really?

Carla: No, not really. They'll hate you because they don't want to be in school, they don't want to learn anything, and they think that you're wasting their time.

Nellie: Oh!

Matt: Here we go.

(Exits)

(From offstage)

Matt: Hey, everyone.

Students: *(Not too enthusiastic.)* Hi. Hey. Hello. Yeah.

Steve: My turn.

(Exits)

(From offstage)

Steve: Hi, kids!

Students: *(Sad, disappointed.)* Oh! Oh, no! Arrragggh!

Carla: I guess I can't wait any longer.

Nellie: Bye.

(Carla Exits)

(From offstage)

Carla: OK, everyone sit down and be quiet!

Students: *(Overjoyed.)* Hey, Hi, Carla! Look – it's Carla! Yay!

(Nellie looks confused. She gathers up her materials, takes a deep breath, and exits.)

Vampire Hunters

CAST:
Vammy
Dr. Hecksing
Gina
Nick

Dr. H: Hello, Vammy. Good to see you again.

Vammy: Good evening, Dr. Hecksing.

(*They shake hands.*)

Dr. H: Your hand is so cold. Are you feeling all right?

Vammy: Perfectly fine, thank you, Dr. Hecksing. I do not have... hot blood.

(*Gina and Nick arrive.*)

Dr. H: OK. I think that's everyone. Are all the members of the Green River Vampire Hunters Club here?

Gina: We're late because we were chasing a vampire!

Nick: It was really scary.

Dr. H: Really? What happened?

Gina: Well, I was with Nick at a coffee shop, and this guy wearing a black coat left. And we left after him, but we didn't see where he went! And then Nick saw a bat!

Nick: I think it was a bat. I'm not sure.

Gina: So we knew that he was a vampire, and turned into a bat! So we tried to follow the bat.

Nick: Maybe it was a bat.

Gina: And we tried to follow it, but it got away.

Vammy: Were there many people in the coffee shop?

Nick: Yeah, a lot of people.

Dr. H: That's good work, anyway. You almost caught a vampire!

Vammy: I don't think the man was a vampire.

Gina: He must be. He turned into a bat!

Nick: Maybe. Or maybe he just turned a corner, and we didn't see him.

Gina: No, he turned into a bat.

Vammy: But why would a vampire go into a coffee shop? Vampires can't drink coffee.

Gina: Maybe he made a mistake.

Dr. H: Maybe he was hunting someone in the coffee shop.

Vammy: But why hunt in a public place? A vampire would wait on a dark street for someone to walk by, not bite someone where everyone can see.

Nick: I think it was just somebody wearing a dark coat.

Gina: No, he was definitely a vampire.

Nick: Maybe.

Dr. H: Next time you think you see a vampire, try to find out if you can see him in a mirror. Vampires cannot be seen in mirrors.

Nick: That's good to know. And then what do we do? Call you?

Gina:	No – you put a wooden stake through its heart!
Nick:	That sounds dangerous.
Vammy:	Yes, very dangerous. It would be better to call all of us, and then we can make a plan.
Dr. H:	Yes, I agree with Vammy. Call us first.
Gina:	But then the vampire might get away!
Nick:	But we will be safer.
Gina:	Who cares about staying safe? We want to kill vampires.
Nick:	We have not had much luck. Every time we find a vampire, he or she gets away.
Dr. H:	Yes, we have had terrible luck.
Gina:	I don't think it's just bad luck.
Dr. H:	What do you mean?
Gina:	I mean that I think someone – someone in this group! – is helping the vampires get away.
Nick:	But why would someone do that?
Vammy:	Yes, there is no reason! It is a silly idea.
Dr. H:	Well, Gina? Why would someone in this group want to help vampires?
Gina:	I think that someone in this group might BE a vampire!
Nick:	No!
Dr. H:	That's hard to believe, Gina.
Nick:	Who could the vampire be?

Gina: Well, let's think about it. Vammy – I never see you in the daytime. Maybe it's because you are a vampire!

Vammy: No, no! You never see me in the daytime because I work at night. So I have to sleep in the daytime.

Dr. H: Where do you work?

Vammy: At the blood bank.

Dr. H.: The blood bank is open at night?

Vammy: Maybe. Some people might need blood at night, don't you think?

Gina: Well, then, maybe it's Nick. Maybe Nick is a vampire!

Nick: Really? Am I? How can I know? Maybe I'm a vampire, and don't know it!

Dr. H: Do you like to drink blood?

Nick: Eeew! No.

Dr. H: Then you can't be a vampire.

Gina: I guess not.

Nick: Oh – that's good! But then – who is the vampire?

Vammy: Maybe none of us is a vampire.

Gina: Someone is helping the vampires get away before we find them! Maybe it's Dr. Hecksing!

Dr. H.: What? I've been hunting vampires for fifty years!

Gina: And maybe one bit you!

Vammy: No vampire would want to bite him! He's so old. His blood is not young and fresh.

Nick:	Let's make sure. Ha! *(Nick brings a cross out his pocket and shows it to Dr. H., who does not react.)*
Dr. H.:	Put that away. I'm not a vampire!
Vammy:	Yes – please put it away!
Nick:	OK. Well, there is only one person left. The vampire must be Gina!
Gina:	No! It's not me!
Nick:	How can we believe you?
Dr. H.:	I have seen Gina walk around in the sunlight many times.
Nick:	Yeah. I have, too. So I guess she can't be a vampire.
Gina:	I told you!
Vammy:	It is like I said. We have no vampires in our group!
Dr. H.:	Then how do the vampires always escape?
Vammy:	I don't know. It is a mystery. We will probably never know the answer.
Nick:	It's very strange.
Vammy:	Just bad luck, maybe.
	(Dr. H.'s phone rings.)
Dr. H.:	Excuse me. *(He talks on the phone for a moment, then hangs up.)* I just heard that there is a large group of vampires in an old house on Pine Street!
Gina:	Really? Let's go!
Nick:	Yes, let's hurry!
	(Dr. H., Nick, and Gina hurry offstage.)

Vammy: I am right behind you! *(He takes out his phone and dials.)* Hello? Vlad? The vampire hunters are coming to your house! .... Yes, that's right! Get out of there, now! *(He hangs up the phone.)* I'm coming, guys! Wait for me!

Ohhh. It would be faster to fly. Oh, well.

(Vammy exits.)

At the Restaurant

CAST:

Waiter: Woody
Friend: Cliff
Husband: Sam
Wife: Diane

SETTING   The Prancing Pony restaurant

(Diane is waiting near the entrance. Sam joins her.)

Diane: Oh. There you are.

Sam: Yes, I am here. Just like we planned.

Diane: I thought you might be late. I thought maybe you had to walk your secretary to her car, or something.

Sam: My secretary is a man, not a woman!

Diane: Yeah, right.

Sam: What did you say?

Diane: Nothing.

Sam: Anyway, how can you talk? I saw the neighbor leaving our house! Handsome, isn't he?

Diane: The window was stuck! He came over to help me with it.

Sam: Yeah, right. I bet he helped with other things, too.

Diane: What did you say?

Sam: Nothing.

(Cliff arrives)

Cliff: Hi, guys! Am I late?

Sam: No, you're right on time. Shall we go in?

Cliff: Sure! I'm hungry.

(Cliff, Sam, and Diane come into the restaurant, and Woody greets them.)

Woody: Hello! Welcome to the Prancing Pony.

Cliff: A table for three, please.

Woody: Of course. Please follow me. *(Woody brings the three customers to a table.)*

Would you like to order some drinks first?

Cliff: Uh, OK. I'd like a Coke, please.

Woody: All right.

Cliff: No, I think an orange juice. Not a Coke.

Woody: Sure thing. And you, ma'am?

Diane: An ice tea.

Sam: A cold drink for a cold heart.

Diane: What did you say?

Sam: Nothing. I'd like a coffee, please.

Woody: OK. Would you like cream or sugar in your coffee?

Diane:	Some sugar might make you sweet.
Sam:	What did you say?
Diane:	Nothing.
Woody:	Sir? Would you like cream or sugar?
Sam:	No, thank you.
Woody:	All right, then. Take a look at our menus, and I will come back with your drinks.
Cliff:	Oh – Um, I think I would like to change my order. I don't want orange juice.
Woody:	I see. What would you like, then?
Cliff:	Ice tea. No – coffee. Wait a minute. I think I want tomato juice.
Woody:	Tomato juice? You're sure?
Cliff:	Yes. Very sure.
Woody:	All right, then. I'll be back with your drinks and to take your orders.

(Woody leaves.)

Cliff:	Look at this menu. A lot of good stuff.
Diane:	We never go anywhere nice. Sam says he's too busy.
Sam:	I AM busy! I have to make money for the family, right?
Diane:	I make money, too.
Sam:	Yeah, right. But I'm the one working to pay the bills.
Diane:	So you were working last Friday night? Until midnight?
Sam:	I had a meeting!

Diane:	Of course you did.
Cliff:	What looks good to you, Sam?
Diane:	Any girl he sees looks good to him.
Sam:	What did you say?
Diane:	Nothing.
Sam:	I'm thinking about getting the fish and chips.
Cliff:	Yeah, that would be good. Or a hamburger. Or maybe a steak.
Diane:	I think I'll get the bacon, lettuce, and tomato sandwich.
Cliff:	Oh – a BLT! Yeah, that sounds good.

(*Woody comes back with drinks.*)

Woody:	Here's your drinks!
Diane:	Thank you.
Cliff:	What's this?
Woody:	That is the tomato juice you asked for.
Cliff:	Tomato juice? Oh, no. I want some hot chocolate, please.
Woody:	Oh. All right. Are you all ready to order?
Diane:	Yes, we're ready to order.
Sam:	She's always ready to order. She loves ordering everyone around.
Diane:	What did you say?
Sam:	Nothing. Um, I'll have the fish and chips.
Woody:	Good. And you?

Diane: The BLT, please. Woody:

          Very good. And you, sir?

Cliff: What will I have? Um, the BLT, also, please.

Woody: Great.

Cliff: Oh – wait. No. I think I'll have a hamburger.

Woody: A hamburger?

Cliff.   That's right.

Sam: You can't seem to decide what you want, Cliff.

Diane: All guys have that problem.

Sam: What did you say?

Diane: Nothing.

Woody: You want a hamburger, right? Are you sure?

Cliff: Yes, I am very sure. Oh, wait. I think I'll have a steak.

Woody: A steak.

Cliff: That's right.

Woody: Are you sure?

Cliff: Of course I'm sure. A steak. Or maybe—

Woody: Yes? You want to change your mind again? Do you?

Cliff: Let me think!

Sam: Someone changes their mind. That sounds familiar.

Diane: What did you say?

Sam:	Nothing.
Cliff:	OK. I have decided. I want a turkey sandwich.
Woody:	Are you sure—
Cliff:	Yes, yes, I am sure! Why do you keep asking me that?
Woody:	I'll bring everything right away.
Diane:	Right away is not soon enough for me.
Sam:	What does that mean?
Diane:	It means I would rather not spend much time with you.
Sam:	Well, I don't want to spend much time with you, either!
Diane:	OK, fine. I'm leaving. You can have dinner with your friend, Cliff.
Sam:	What do you mean, my friend? Cliff is your friend, not mine! And I'm leaving too!

(Sam and Diane leave.)

Cliff:	Huh.

(Woody returns with the food.)

Woody:	All right. Here's the BLT, the fish and chips, and the turkey sandwich. And here's your hot chocolate.
Cliff:	I don't think I want a turkey sandwich. I guess I'll have this BLT. And I don't want a hot chocolate. I'll just have water.
Woody:	Are your friends coming back?
Cliff:	I don't think so. But that's OK. I'm hungry. Hmm. Maybe instead of the BLT I will have these fish and chips. And instead of water, I'll have a beer.
Woody:	And will you want dessert after dinner?

Cliff:	Yes. An ice cream sundae, please.
Woody:	Very well.
Cliff:	No, wait – some cherry pie instead.
Woody:	Cherry pie?
Cliff:	No, no, not cherry pie. I want some chocolate cake.
Woody:	Chocolate cake. All right.
Cliff:	No, no – wait. I need to think about this.
Woody:	We're going to be here all night, aren't we?
Cliff:	Yeah, probably.
Woody:	I'll just bring all the desserts!
Cliff:	Perfect! I love this place. I think I'll come here more often.
Woody:	Oh. Next time, come here on a Tuesday or Wednesday.
Cliff:	Why Tuesday or Wednesday?
Woody:	Because those are my days off!
Cliff:	OK. I'll come on Wednesday.
Woody:	Great!
Cliff:	Or maybe Friday.
Woody:	Uooggh!
Cliff:	It might take me a while to decide what I want. You should sit down. Here's a menu. You should order something while you wait.

(Woody looks at the menu. After a long pause, Cliff speaks again.)

Cliff:	Well? What do you want?
Woody:	Oh… I just can't decide!

Time for Love

CAST:

Husband: Harry
Wife: Wendy
Friend: Frank
Harry's Aunt: Dee

SETTING: A restaurant. Harry and Wendy are at a small table.

Wendy: Oh, I'm not sure, Frank.

Harry: Please! Listen – I love you! I love you so much! I want to spend my life making you happy. Marry me!

Wendy: Are you sure you will be happy with me?

Harry: Of course I will be happy! I will do anything you say! I will do everything for you! I will think about you every minute – every second!

Wendy: Are you sure?

Harry: Yes, yes, I am sure! I will make you so happy, Wendy. I promise!

Wendy: Well, maybe…

Harry: Just say yes! Say that you will marry me!

Wendy: Well, all right. Yes, Harry! I will marry you!

Harry: Oh, my darling! We will be happy forever!

FIVE YEARS LATER

SETTING: Harry's house. Harry is sitting, and Frank is standing.

Frank: Hey, Harry. Let's go out and do something.

Harry: Like what?

Frank: I don't know. How about the art museum? You told me that your wife wanted to go. She could come with us. That might be fun.

Harry: That's boring. I just want to sit in front of the TV and drink beer.

(Throws empty beer can on the *floor.*)

Frank: At least you could clean up after yourself.

(Enter Wendy)

Wendy: Harry! Hey, Harry! Harry!

Harry: What?

Wendy: You said you were going to wash the dishes three days ago. But the dishes are still dirty.

Harry: I'll do it later.

Wendy: But we don't have any clean dishes for dinner tonight.

Harry: So what? We can just get a pizza. See? No dishes, no problem!

Wendy: Pizza? Again? Why don't you just wash the dishes?

Harry: I said I will do it later! I'm watching TV!

Wendy: You always say that. But you never do it.

Harry: I will do it later! Leave me alone!

(Wendy leaves)

Frank: Uh, maybe I should go home.

Harry: Why?

Frank: I think you need to talk to your wife.

Harry: Oh, I hate talking to her. You know something, Frank? I wish I had never married her!

Frank: Wendy's nice, Harry. When she said she would marry you, you were so happy! Remember?

Harry: Yeah, I thought she was great.

Frank: Well, she's beautiful and smart. You're lucky to be married to her. I wish I was!

Harry: You can have her! Sure, she looks nice, but she is also really unfair. She always wants me to clean the house or wash the car or cut the grass. I shouldn't have married her.

Frank: I think you should talk to her. You have to find a way to make your marriage better.

(Dee Dee enters the room.)

Frank: Oh. Hello?

Dee Dee: Yes, yes, hello, hello, I say. Hello!

Harry: Oh, Frank, this is my aunt Dee Dee. She is staying with us for a while.

Frank: Nice to meet you. I'm Frank.

Dee Dee: Frank. Frank? OK, Frank. Yes, yes. Frank. I am Dee. Yes. I am looking for a subject.

Frank: A subject?

Dee Dee: Yes, a subject. You know what a subject is, I hope? A subject for my experiment. A volunteer.

Frank: Aunt Dee Dee, you're always coming up with strange ideas.

Harry: What kind of experiment?

Dee Dee: *(Dee Dee shows them an armband.)* This. It's a time band.

Harry: What's a time band?

Dee Dee: It lets you travel in time.

Frank: Yeah, right! Travel in time!

Harry: Really?

Dee Dee: I think so. Yes, I think so. You put it on, see, and type in the date you want to visit. And the machine will put your mind into your mind when you were younger, or older.

Frank: Pretty hard to believe, Aunt Dee Dee.

Harry: So your body doesn't really travel in time. Just your mind?

Dee Dee: Yes, yes, just the mind. The mind. And the time band. That travels, too.

Frank: Wow. That's amazing.

Harry: Yeah, but only if it works. Hey, Harry – imagine that I could go back in time, and stop myself from marrying Wendy! Oh, that would be sweet!

Frank: So why don't you try it?

Dee Dee: Here, I will place the time band on your arm. Like this. Type in the date you want to visit.

Harry: Well, I don't know. It might be dangerous.

Dee Dee: Oh, yes, very dangerous. Very, very dangerous. What date do you want to visit?

Harry: Well, if I could visit a time in the past, I would choose – yeah, the day I asked Wendy to marry me. So I put in the date like this? *(Types.)*

Dee Dee: That's it! Bye, bye!

FIVE YEARS EARLIER

SETTING: A restaurant

Wendy: Are you sure?

Harry: Huh? Where am I? Sure about what?

Wendy: You just asked me to marry you.

Harry: Oh, yeah. Hey! It worked! It's five years ago!

Wendy: Huh?

Harry: It's five years ago, and I can change my life! No, Wendy, I don't want to marry you! I really don't!

Wendy: What? Then why did you ask me?

Harry: Whoo, hoo! I'm free! I'm not married to you anymore! Life is going to be perfect!

Wendy: You're crazy! You ask me to marry you, then tell me you don't want to marry me – I'm getting out of here!

Harry: Yeah! Bye. bye, baby! I hope I never see you again!

Wendy: Arrghh!

(She leaves.)

Harry: Oh, I feel so good! When I go back to my life in the future, everything is going to be so great. I didn't marry Wendy, so I can use all my money on myself. I'll probably have a cool apartment, and lots of beautiful girlfriends. Oh, it's going to be great! Here I go. *(Types.)*

FIVE YEARS EARLIER

SETTING: Harry's house.

Harry: I'm home again! I'm – hey, what's this? My same old crappy house? It looks even worse now! Maybe the time machine didn't work. I'm probably still married to Wendy. Wendy! Hey, Wendy!

(Wendy enters)

Wendy: Hi!

Harry: Yeah, I thought so. Still married!

Wendy: Of course I'm still married! Frank? Where are you, Frank?

(Frank enters)

Frank: Here I am, sweetheart!

Harry: 'Sweetheart'?

Frank: I put all our bags into your car, Harry. Thanks again for agreeing to drive us to the airport. *(Quietly)* I'll give you a few bucks. I know you lost your job.

Harry: I lost my job?

Wendy: I can't wait. In a few hours we'll be in Paris!

Frank: Like on our honeymoon!

Wendy: Oh, honey! This is such a wonderful anniversary present!

Harry: Hey, what's going on?

Frank: What do you mean?

Harry: I mean, I live in this terrible house, and you're married to each other, and I lost my job?

Wendy: Cheer up, Harry. I'm sure your luck will get better soon.

Harry: Do you guys think I am a happy person?

Frank: Well, not happy, exactly. But like Wendy said, your luck will get better soon.

Harry: It's going to get better right now! I have a time machine here, that I got from my aunt Dee Dee, and I am going to fix this! I'm going to go back to the restaurant on the night I asked you to marry me.

Wendy: Yes, you asked me to marry you, and then you changed your mind! "Bye. bye, baby! I hope I never see you again!" That's what you said!

Harry: I was wrong, and this time I will change it back to the way it was before!

Wendy: But I am happy, so happy, with Frank! You can't change my life!

Harry: I can, and I will! The next time I see you, we will be married! *(Types on his time band.)*

FIVE YEARS EARLIER

SETTING: A restaurant

Harry: I do want to marry you, Wendy! I know my life will be terrible without you!

Wendy: Oh, Harry, I'm sorry. But you don't understand something.

Harry:	No, no – I was wrong before! I was so stupid! I didn't understand how lucky I was, to have such a wonderful wife! But now I understand! Our lives will be so good!
Wendy:	No, no, you don't understand. You see, I've been talking to this woman.

(Dee Dee enters.)

Dee Dee:	Yes, hello, hello.
Harry:	Aunt Dee Dee? What are you doing here?
Wendy:	She came to see me, Harry. She found out about your plan, and came back in time to warn me.
Dee Dee:	Yes. My nephew, Harry, is not a good man, Wendy. He will not be a good husband.
Harry:	But – but I can change! I can make you happy!
Wendy:	Forget it, Harry. I will have a terrible future with you, but Dee Dee told me that I will be very happy with Frank.
Dee Dee:	Frank is a good man. A good husband.
Harry:	You can't do this!
Wendy:	I have already done it, Harry. I've made my decision. You're out of time!
Harry:	Nooo!

Why I Need More Money

CAST:
Rich student: Brett
Poor student: Vic
Brett's Mother: Mom
Brett's Father: Dad
Brett's Brother: Brock
Brett's Grandmother

SETTING: A living room. Brett and Vic are sitting in chairs.

Brett: Oh, I'm full.

Vic: You're not going to throw the rest of the food away, are you?

Brett: Why not? I'm full.

Vic: You could save it for later…

(Brett throws leftover food in the garbage.)

…or give it to me, if you don't want it.

Brett: Oh, sorry! I didn't know you wanted it.

Vic: That's OK. I think I have some ramen noodles or something.

Brett: Uh-huh.

(He picks up and leafs through a magazine.)

Oh, look at the new Maserati! That is a nice car!

Vic: Yes, very nice. And very expensive. You could buy ten regular cars for the same price.

Brett:	Who wants a regular car? If I had this car, oh, the girls would love me. Everybody would watch me drive by!
Vic:	You have a really nice car already.
Brett:	It's OK, but it's almost a year old! I really need a new one. I really need this Maserati!
Vic:	Then what would you do with your old car?
Brett:	Throw it away! Who cares! Look at the picture – isn't that a great car? What kind of car do you want?
Vic:	A car? Oh, I don't care. Just something I can use for a long time. I have to take the bus every day to school. I spend almost three hours a day on the bus. If I had a car, I could spend more time on homework.
Brett:	Yeah, that's a good idea. I can tell my parents I need a new, fast car so I can spend more time on homework!
Vic:	I never see you do homework. You have a lot of time, but you don't study. You go to the casino, or the nightclub, or shopping for new watches, or expensive restaurants.
Brett:	Yeah, but my parents don't know that. I'm going to call them now.
	(He dials the phone.)
	(Grandmother appears on the stage.)
Grand:	Hello? Hello? Who is this?
Brett:	Grandma? Hi. It's Brett.
Grand:	Brett? Oh, OK. Let me call him. *(Towards offstage)* Brett? Brett? Telephone, Brett!
Brett:	No, no, Grandma! It's me! I'm Brett!

Grand:	I'm sorry. I don't think Brett is home now. You will have to call back later.
Brett:	I'm Brett! Can I talk to Dad?
Grand:	You should listen to me. I told you, Brett is not home. I'm not sure where he is. Maybe you should talk to his father instead.
Brett:	Yes. Fine. Let me talk to my Dad.
Grand:	You don't understand. You need to talk to Brett's father, not YOUR father.

(Father appears on the stage.)

Oh, son. There's someone on the phone. I think you should talk to him.

Father:	Hello?
Brett:	Hi, Dad? It's me, Brett.
Father:	Oh, hi! Just a second. Let me put you on speakerphone so your mom can talk, too. *(To mother.)* Come here – it's Brett.

(Mother joins Father and Grandmother on the stage.)

Mother:	Brett? How are you? Are you OK?
Brett:	Hi, Mom. Actually, I have a problem.
Mother:	Oh, no! What happened?
Father:	Did you get in an accident?
Mother:	I told you to be careful!
Brett:	No, no, nothing like that.
Mother:	Then, what is it?
Brett:	I just need a new car, that's all.

Father:	Oh, OK. I was worried! A new car? How much do you need?
Mother:	Wait a minute – why do you need a new car?
Brett:	Well, the car I have now is getting old, and if I get a new one I could get to school faster, and get home faster, and have more time for homework.
Father:	That's a good idea!

(Brock wanders onto the stage)

Brock:	Brett's getting a new car? I want a car!
Father:	Oh, well, OK. Here's some money. You can—
Mother:	*(Slaps Father's hand.)* *(To Brock)* You don't need a new car, Brock! You're not even in high school!
Brock:	Oh, this is so unfair!

(Brock wanders away.)

Brett:	Hello? So, anyway, I've heard the new Maserati is fast.
Father:	Ooh, a Maserati! They're good cars. How much do you need?
Mother:	Now, now, just wait. I don't understand. Your old car is still working, right?
Brett:	Well, yeah. It works OK, I guess.
Mother:	It was a very expensive car, wasn't it?
Brett:	Well, a little expensive, I guess.
Mother:	So, why do you need a new one?
Brett:	I told you – to save time so I can do more homework.
Father:	He needs to do his homework, dear.

(Brock wanders onto the stage) Brock:

Hey, Dad. I need a new cellphone.

Father: You do? Well, here, take some money.

Mother: *(Slaps Father's hand.)* *(To Brock)* Why do you need a new phone, Brock?

Brock: My phone is so old! I got it three months ago!

Father: Then I guess you need a new one. Here—

Mother: *(Slaps Father's hand.)* *(To Brock)* You do not need a new phone, Brock!

Brock: Oh, man! This is so unfair!

(Brock wanders away.)

Mother: You don't need an expensive new car to do homework!

Brett: But it would help.

Father: Yes, it would help him, dear.

Mother: What about your roommate? He gets good grades, right?

Brett: Vic? Yeah, he gets good grades.

Mother: Does he have an expensive new car?

Brett: Well, he's right here, Mom, if you want to ask him.

Mother: Oh, he's there? Vic? Can you hear me, Vic?

Vic: Yes, hello.

Mother: This is Brett's mother.

Father: And father.

Vic:	Nice to talk to you.
Mother:	Brett told me that you get really good grades.
Vic:	Yes, sometimes. It's a lot of work.
Mother:	Tell me, Vic, do you have an expensive new car?
Brett:	*(To Vic)* Tell her that you do!
Vic:	*(To Brett)* I'm not going to lie to your mother! *(To Mother)* No, I don't have an expensive new car.
Father:	What kind of car do you have?
Vic:	I don't have any car. I don't have enough money. I take the bus to school.
Father:	The bus? That's a long way! It must take a lot of time.
Vic:	Yes, it does. But it's OK. I have a bus pass, so it's not too expensive.
Mother:	Brett, why don't you take the bus? Then you wouldn't need any car at all!
Brett:	But – but – I need a car!
Mother:	What for?
Brett:	To go to school, and, uh – shopping for food. Yeah – I need a car to go shopping for food! You don't want me to die, do you?
Vic:	I just walk to the store. It's only a few miles away.
Father:	A few miles! No, no, that's no good.
	(Brock wanders onto the stage) Brock:
	Hey, Dad. I need a pencil for school.
Father:	You do? Well, here, take some money.

Mother: *(Slaps Father's hand.) (To Brock)* No! You don't need – wait – I don't even know what you want now! What is it? What do you want this time? A car? A phone? A motorcycle? What?

Brock: Just a pencil, for school.

Father: That's fine. Here—

Mother: *(Slaps Father's hand.)* Oh, wait. I'm sorry. Yes, go ahead and give him the money for a pencil.

Brock: Wow! Thanks, Dad! Thanks, Mom!

(Brock exits.)

Mother: Brett, back to you. I don't think you need a new car. Your old one is fine.

Brett: But – Mom, I need a new car! You don't understand my life.

Mother: Understand what?

Brett: If I had a new car, a Maserati, all the girls would love me!

Father: Oh, that's true. He has a good point, dear. Boys have to think about that. I mean, he's not going to get a girl any other way.

Mother: You need a car to get girls?

Brett: Sure!

Mother: Vic, do you have a girlfriend?

Vic: Yes, I do. I've been dating her for about six months.

Brett: *(To Vic)* Shut up!

Father: Oh, that's nice. Is she pretty?

Vic: Yes, she is. And smart, too.

Mother: Does she go to school, too?

Vic:	Yes, she does. We ride the bus together. Of course, maybe we can't do that much longer.
Mother:	Why not? What's the problem?
Vic:	Well, I may have to drop out of school for a while, to make some money.
Father:	Why do you need money? To get a nice car?
Vic:	No, I need money to pay for school.
Brett:	Yeah, that's nice. So, Father, you can just put the money in my bank account, right?
Father:	Well, I don't know, son. I guess I'm not sure if you really need—
Mother:	I do know! Brett, you're not getting money for a new car!
Brett:	Father, can you talk to Mother? You understand, right?
Father:	I am beginning to understand a lot of things. Just a moment, son. Your mother and grandmother want to talk to me.
	(Mother, Father, and Grandmother hold a whispered conversation.)
Father:	*(Finally)* But he needs a car to get a girlfriend.
Grand:	YOU didn't need a car to get THIS girl! And she's the best thing that ever happened to you!
Father:	So – no car?
Mother:	No car!
Grand:	No, no, I have a better idea – listen! *(Whispers to Father and Mother)*
Mother:	Good idea!
Grand:	It will teach my grandson a good lesson!

Brett:	Father? Hello? Hello? Are you there? *(To Vic)* Why did you have to tell them about your problems? You are so selfish! Now, they are not thinking about me!
Vic:	I'm not going to tell lies.
Father:	Hello? Brett, are you there?
Brett:	Yes, Father I'm here.
Father:	Your mother and grandmother and I have talked, and we need the bank account information so we can transfer the money.
Brett:	*(Off the phone)* Yes! I'm getting the new car! *(To phone)* OK, Father. But why? You already know my bank account information.
Mother:	No, no, you don't understand, dear. We want Vic's bank account information, not yours.
Brett:	Vic's bank account?
Mother:	Yes – we want to help him out.
Vic:	Oh, please, you don't have to do that!
Father:	We want to! We want you go get a new car, and stay in school. And you'll have some money to take your girlfriend to some nice places.
Mother:	Let us do that for you, Vic. It would make us so happy.
Brett:	But – but –
Vic:	Well, thank you! Thank you so much!
Father:	Please send us the information.
Vic:	I will! Thank you, again! I'll pay you back as soon as I can!
Mother:	You're very welcome! Goodbye, now. Goodbye, Brett! We'll talk to you again soon!

Brett:	Wait! I didn't want to tell you, but I need a new car because I had an accident! The old one doesn't work anymore!
Mother:	We'll send you the money for a bus pass, dear. Will that help?
Grand:	That's a good idea. A bus pass!
Brett:	A bus pass? But – but—
Father:	Goodbye, son! Goodbye, Vic!
Vic:	Goodbye!
Brett:	But – but—
Father:	Goodbye! *(Father hangs up the phone.)*
	(Father, Mother, and Grandmother exit the stage.)
Brett:	I don't believe this!
Vic:	No – I don't believe it, either!
Brett:	Hey – I have an idea. You're going to get a lot of money, right?
Vic:	I guess so.
Brett:	So YOU can buy the Maserati, and I can borrow it! Good idea, right?
Vic:	A Maserati? No way! I'll just get an old Honda or something. *(Vic starts to walk away.)*
Brett:	No, no, wait! A new Maserati would be really nice…
Vic:	I don't need a Maserati!
Brett:	But – But –
	(Vic exits, followed by Brett.)

Psychiatric Help 5¢

CAST:
Doctor: Dee
Patients: Sam
            Holly
            Rita
            Ron
2 Hospital Attendants

Dee: Psychiatric help, here! Only five cents! Psychiatric help! Come and get it!

Sam: Did you say "psychiatric help"?

Dee: That's right.

Sam: For only five cents.

Dee: Exactly.

Sam: Wow. Well, maybe I can talk to you about my problem. It's only five cents, so what can I lose? You see, I feel—

Dee: Hold it. Wait a second. Five cents, please.

Sam: Oh, Here you are.

(*Sam gives Dee five cents. Dee barks like a dog.*)

Dee: OK now you can talk.

Sam: It's just that I feel so much pressure. So much stress.

Dee: Problems at home?

Sam:	No, home is fine. But I feel a lot of stress at school. And I have a job after school, and that gives me stress, too.
Dee:	I see. Tell me about your school stress.
Sam:	I want to be a top student, you know? So I study hard. When my friends ask me to go to a movie, I tell them I need to study. When my friends invite me to a party, I tell them I need to study. I never have any fun.
Dee:	Has all your studying made you a top student?
Sam:	No, not the top. I mean, I get good grades, but I'm not the best.
Dee:	And did you say that you also get stress from work?
Sam:	Yes, I do.
Dee:	What do you do?
Sam:	It's just an after-school job. I'm a waiter at a restaurant. But people get so angry if the food is slow, or if something is wrong. Sometimes, nothing is wrong, but they change their minds, and then they blame me! Also, I don't even get much money.
	(Holly enters, looks at the booth.) Dee:
	That doesn't sound like too much fun.
Sam:	It isn't!
Dee:	You have a lot of stress from school, and a lot of stress from work. But I have the answer to all your problems.
Sam:	Great! What should I do?
Dee:	It's easy. Just quit.
Sam:	Quit?
Dee:	Yeah. Quit school, and quit work. Then you won't have any stress.

Sam:	But if I quit work, I won't have any money! How can I buy food? And if I quit school, I won't have a good job in the future!
Dee:	Those are new problems. If you want me to help you with those problems, you have to pay five cents again.
Sam:	No, thank you.
	(Sam leaves.)
Dee:	Next!
Holly:	Um, hi?
Dee:	Psychiatric help is five cents. Do you need some help?
	(Rita enters.)
Holly:	Well, maybe. I just feel so bad. You see—
Dee:	Five cents, please.
Holly:	Oh, of course.
	(Holly pays Dee five cents. Dee barks like a dog.)
Holly:	Are you OK?
Dee:	I'm all right. You said you feel bad?
Holly:	Yes, I really do. You see, I come from China. This is the first time I lived in another country. Everything is strange – the school, the weather, the food, the language. But most of all, I really miss my family. I miss my home. I just feel so bad.
Dee:	Well, your problem is easy to fix.
Holly:	Really? You can make me happy here in America?
Dee:	No. My advice is to quit school and go back home. Then you'll be happy.

Holly:	Quit school? But—
Dee:	Listen, I told you the answer to your problem. Please let the next person get my help.
Holly:	You weren't any help at all! You watch – I'll be fine here!
	(Holly leaves.)
Dee:	Next!
Rita:	Hi. I heard you give psychiatric help for just five cents?
Dee:	That's right.
Rita:	Good, because I need someone to talk to. You see, I have a boyfriend, and he—
Dee:	Wait a second. Five cents, please.
Rita:	Oh, yeah.
	(Rita gives Dee five cents. Dee barks like a dog.)
	Are you all right?
Dee:	I'm fine. So, what's the problem?
Rita:	I have this boyfriend.
Dee:	Oh, good for you!
Rita:	Yeah, but I'm not sure he is good for me. He forgot my birthday last week.
Dee:	Everyone forgets things sometimes.
Rita:	OK, but he always comes late when we have a date. And he says he doesn't want me to spend time with my friends.
Dee:	I see.

Rita:	And I am pretty sure he has other girlfriends. I saw pictures of him kissing other girls on his phone, and my friend saw him with another girl yesterday.
Dee:	You looked at his phone? You shouldn't do that.
Rita:	I know it was wrong. But what should I do? I can't trust him, and I don't think he loves me at all!
Dee:	Hey – you have a boyfriend! Lots of girls don't have a boyfriend. You should feel lucky.
Rita:	Lucky? But he is a liar and he is not nice!

(Ron enters and stands behind Rita.)

Dee:	No one's perfect. You need to keep him.
Rita:	I think a boyfriend should respect his girlfriend.
Dee:	I told you what you should do. There's someone waiting behind you. Next!
Ron:	*(To Rita)* I'm sorry. I didn't mean to interrupt.
Rita:	Oh, no, I just…
Ron:	If you're not finished, I can wait.
Rita:	No, no, that's OK. You go ahead.
Ron:	You're sure?
Rita:	Yes, yes, I'm sure. Nice meeting you.
Ron:	Really nice to meet you, too!
Dee:	If you want my help, give me five cents.
Ron:	Oh, OK.

(Rita reluctantly leaves.)

	(To Rita) **Um, bye.** *(Ron gives Dee the money. Dee barks like a dog.)*
Ron:	That's a strange sound.
Dee:	We're not talking about me. What's your problem?
Ron:	Well, it's kind of embarrassing.
Dee:	Don't waste my time. Just tell me.
Ron:	Well, I think I'm a nice guy, and not too ugly…
Dee:	You're all right.
Ron:	…but I never meet any girls. I can't get a girlfriend.
Dee:	Don't worry about it. If you have a girlfriend, you will have to spend lots of money. Taking her to dinner, buying her presents, giving her flowers. You're lucky you are alone.
Ron:	I don't feel lucky. I would love to remember a girl's birthday, and give her flowers. Like that girl that you were just talking to. Wow, she was so beautiful.
Dee:	She already has a boyfriend, so leave her alone.
Ron:	So what should I do?
Dee:	Nothing. Be happy you're alone.
	(Two hospital attendants appear behind Ron.)
Ron:	That doesn't sound like good advice.
Attend.1:	There she is!
Attend. 2:	Yes, that's her. Get her!
	(The attendants try to capture Dee, while she tries to evade them)
Ron:	What? Hey! What's going on?

Attend. 1:	Get her!
Ron:	What are you doing to the doctor?

(The attendants succeed in grabbing Dee.)

Attend. 2:	She is not a doctor.
Ron:	She isn't?
Attend. 1:	No – she escaped from the hospital! She is a crazy person!
Ron:	Crazy?
Attend. 1:	Come on, Dee.
Attend. 2:	Back to the hospital with you!
Dee:	No – no! I'm not crazy!

(Dee begins barking like a dog as the attendants leave with her.)

Ron:	Wow!

(Rita enters, looking offstage where Dee has been taken. She doesn't notice Ron, and bumps into him.)

Rita:	Oh – sorry!
Ron:	That's all right.
Rita:	Is it true? She was crazy?
Ron:	Yes, it's true. She gave me some crazy advice.
Rita:	Me, too. My name is Rita, by the way.
Ron:	Hi, Rita. I'm Ron.
Rita:	Hi. Well, I guess I should go. Bye.

Ron: Bye. No, wait a minute. Rita?

Rita: Yes?

Ron: Um... Would you like to have lunch with me?

Rita: Well... sure!

(Rita and Ron leave together.)

Vacation Plans

CAST:
Nessa
Bridget
Charlene
Ophelia

Ophelia: I can't believe the quarter is finally ending.

Charlene: Yes. I am so sick of grammar and reading. But now summer vacation is coming soon!

Bridget: So – where are you guys going on your summer vacation? I can't decide between Paris or Tahiti.

Nessa: Where's Tahiti?

Bridget: It's an island in the Pacific Ocean. Beautiful beaches and palm trees.

Nessa: I bet the plane ticket will be expensive.

Bridget: We only get one summer vacation a year. You can't worry about money. Spend as much as you want and have a good time!

Nessa: You can't spend money you don't have. I don't think I will be going to Tahiti.

Bridget: Too bad for you.

Charlene: Where do you want to go, then? We should all go together! That would be a lot of fun.

Nessa: Yeah – good idea! But where should we go?

Ophelia:	I don't know. Maybe Disneyland?
Bridget:	Disneyland? Oh, please! Everyone goes to Disneyland. That's so boring.
Charlene:	I think we should go to Hawaii.
Nessa:	You just want to go to Hawaii because Jimmy is going there. I heard him and some of the other boys talking about it.
Charlene:	I don't care where Jimmy is going! Hawaii is really nice. Beaches, and warm weather, and, um, pineapples. They have pineapples, right?
Nessa:	And Jimmy can see you in a bikini.
Charlene:	I don't care about that! He can look if he wants. I don't care.
Nessa:	Jimmy is kind of cute.
Charlene:	Yeah – isn't he?
Bridget:	Jimmy's friend Tom is the cute one. Is he going to Hawaii with Jimmy?
Nessa:	I don't think so. He usually goes with Jimmy, but I heard him say that he hates Hawaii because he gets terrible sunburns.
Bridget:	Well, I'm not going to Hawaii, either. I've already been to Hawaii. Many times. It's boring.
Ophelia:	Maybe we could go camping in the mountains. That might be fun.
Nessa:	That sounds good. But I don't have a sleeping bag.
Bridget:	So just buy one. What's the problem?
Nessa:	I don't have a lot of extra money.
Ophelia:	I bet you can borrow a sleeping bag from your host family.
Nessa:	I can ask them. Maybe they have a tent, too.

Bridget: Who wants to spend summer vacation in a tent in the forest, with bugs and bears and dirt?

Charlene: And a campfire. That would be so romantic.

Ophelia: I love camping. Sitting next to a river, and walking in the forest, and eating hot dogs over a fire.

Bridget: I'd rather stay in a nice hotel with a pool.

Nessa: Do you want to invite Jimmy on our camping trip?

Charlene: Oh – do you think he would come?

Nessa: I was joking!

Charlene: Oh. Yeah, I knew that. Ha, ha! But you know, he might want to come.

Ophelia: So, do we all agree? A camping trip?

Charlene: Sure.

Nessa: I'd like to go, yeah. How about it, Bridget? Want to come with us?

Ophelia: No, Bridget doesn't want to go camping. She wants to go someplace expensive and far away.

Nessa: Come on, Bridget. It'll be fun.

Charlene: Yeah, come with us.

Bridget: No way. Camping in the forest? With bugs and bears and spiders? I'm going to Tahiti.

Ophelia: Oh, please come with us! We would miss you if you didn't come!

Charlene: It will be fun, Bridget!

Nessa: Please, Bridget? Please?

Bridget: I said no. There is no way I'm going to go camping!

Ophelia: Excuse me. I need to make a phone call.

(Ophelia goes behind the others and makes a call. We cannot hear what she says.)

Charlene: I know a place with a beautiful waterfall, and we can walk in the forest. It's very peaceful.

Nessa: And we can have a campfire at night! We can eat hot dogs and tell ghost stories. So much fun!

Bridget: Forget it. I'll never go camping.

(Ophelia returns)

Ophelia: Guess what? I just called Jimmy!

Charlene: You did WHAT?

Ophelia: Yeah. And he says he would love to go camping with us.

Charlene: He did? Oh!

Bridget: You have fun with Jimmy on your stupid camping trip. I'll be at a nice hotel.

Ophelia: And Jimmy says that Tom can come, too.

Bridget: Tom's coming? Well, I guess I could go camping. It would be better to go to Tahiti in the winter, anyway. But I am going to sleep in my own tent. The biggest tent.

Ophelia: Fine – but that means you have to carry it.

Bridget: Can't we – I don't know. Can't we hire someone to carry our stuff for us?

Ophelia: That would ruin the whole idea of camping!

Bridget: Oh, OK.

Ophelia: Let's go find a sleeping bag for Nessa.

Bridget: Nessa, I will buy a sleeping bag for you if you agree to carry my stuff.

Nessa: You can carry your own stuff, Bridget!

Charlene: Or ask Tom to help you.

Bridget: Oh, shut up!

Do you think he would do that?

(Lots of teasing as everyone exits.)

Star-Crossed Lovers

CAST:
Boy: Rob
Girl: Julie
Boy's Friend: George
Girl's Friend: Bev

SETTING: The Mall. Rob and George are shopping, and behind and to the side are Julie and Bev.

George: Come on, Rob. I can't find anything I like. Let's go get lunch.

Rob: Yeah, OK. *(He sees Julie)* Hey – who's that?

George: Who?

Rob: Her! Over there. The most beautiful girl in the world!

George: That girl in the white shirt? Oh, dude, that's Julie. But you don't want to get close to her!

Rob: Why not? Is it because you like her, too? Is that it?

George: She's dangerous.

Rob: Dangerous? Why? Because she breaks every guy's heart with her beauty?

George: No, no! Don't you know? Her dad is the president of Highline College!

Rob: You're kidding!

George: No, I'm not. And your mom is the president of Green River. She would never allow you to date a girl from Highline! She would boil you in water to make soup!

Rob: Maybe I won't tell her.

George: She will find out, and then you will be in big, big trouble. You know that Highline and Green River are enemies. We hate them, and they hate us. Your mom would kill you if your girlfriend is the Highline president's daughter! She would burn you in a fire!

Rob: But – she's so beautiful!

George: Come on. There are lots of beautiful girls. Lots of lovely girls that are not from Highline.

Rob: You don't understand. I love her!

George: You don't even know her. You haven't even talked to her yet. How can you love her?

Rob: I just know that I do.

George: Come on!

(Rob and George go upstage. Julie and Bev move downstage.)

Julie: Who was that? Do you know that boy's name?

Bev: Stop staring! It's embarrassing!

Julie: But he's so cute! I love his hair.

Bev: He's not that cute. Besides, you can never date him.

Julie: Do you think he doesn't like me? Oh!

Bev: Oh, I think he likes you, all right. He was staring at you, too. But your dad would never want you to date him.

Julie: Why not?

Bev:	Because that's Rob. His mom is the president of Green River!
Julie:	You're kidding! Green River?
Bev:	Yep. And your dad would kill you if you dated the son of the president of Green River! He would cut off all of your fingers and toes!
Julie:	Eeew, Green River. That's disgusting. But – his hair is really cute. I think – I think I love him!
Bev:	Oh, get out. You saw him one time.
Julie:	No, I do – I love him!
Bev:	Forget it. You can never date him. Your dad would kill you. Julie:
	He won't kill me if he doesn't know. Bev – you have to help me!
Bev:	Help you? Help you get killed?
Julie:	No, no – help me meet Bob! Oh, how I love his name. Bob, Bob, Bob!
Bev:	Rob. His name is Rob.
Julie:	Yeah, Rob! I love that name. He has cute hair. You've got to help me!
Bev:	It's dangerous!
Julie:	I don't care if it's dangerous. And if you are my friend, you will help me.
Bev:	Oh – OK. I'll help you get killed. What do you want me to do?
Julie:	It's easy. Let's go over there, and then you talk to the other boy, Rob's friend, and let me be alone with Rob.
Bev:	Well, OK. And then after that, when your dad kills you, I will come to your funeral.
Julie:	Great! Let's go.

(Julie and Bev join Rob and George in the middle of the stage.)

Bev: Hi. I'm Bev.

George: Oh, hi, Bev. I'm George.

Bev: I know this is strange, but, um, can you help me?

George: Help you with what?

Bev: Well, I, um – I need help with… Um. Oh! I know! Yeah. I want to try on some clothes, and maybe you could tell me which ones look good on me.

George: You want me to tell if your clothes look good?

Bev: That's right. You know, a guy's idea. My girlfriends tell me what they like, but I want to know what boys think.

Rob: Go! Go help her, George!

George: Uh, OK, I guess.

Bev: Great! Over here!

(Bev and George leave.)

Rob: Hi. I'm Rob.

Julie: I'm Julie.

Rob: I'm really glad you came over. I really wanted to meet you.

Julie: Really? Why?

Rob: You're the most beautiful girl I have ever seen!

Julie: Oh – thank you! I wanted to meet you, too!

Rob: Wow! Maybe we can go on a date sometime?

Julie: Sure – any time, anywhere!

Rob: Great! But I have to tell you something.

Julie: What?

Rob: It's a terrible thing.

Julie: What? What's so terrible?

Rob: I heard your father is the president of Highline College.

Julie: That's right.

Rob: Well, my mom is the president of Green River College.

Julie: Yes – I heard.

Rob: What do you think? It will be difficult for us to be together.

Julie: Yes, I know. But – I don't care! I just don't care! I know that I love you!

Rob: I know that I love you, too! I don't care about my mom, or your dad! They will have to accept our love!

Julie: Yes! After we get married, they will accept us.

Rob: Especially after we have children.

Julie: Children?

Rob: Right. We will have three or four kids. Maybe five.

Julie: I don't know if I want so many kids.

Rob: It will be great! We'll take them to baseball games.

Julie: I hate baseball! But maybe we can have one kid, and she can learn to play the piano. That will be perfect.

Rob: Piano? No, no. Maybe guitar. Or drums! That will be cool.

Julie: No, it has to be the piano. And we can take family vacations to Italy

	and France.
Rob:	Europe's boring.
Julie:	But they have the best art museums!
Rob:	Art? Who cares about art museums? We can take our family vacations in Auburn. Or maybe Kent.
Julie:	That's so boring!

(There is a pause.)

What kind of music do you like?

Rob:	Hip hop.
Julie:	I like classical.
Rob:	What kind of movies do you like?
Julie:	Romantic movies.
Rob:	Oh, really? I like action movies. And horror movies about guys with big knives.
Julie:	Oh, no! Well, what kind of food do you like?
Rob:	Oh, you know. Pizza, hamburgers. How about you?
Julie:	I like sushi and kimchi.
Rob:	Ugghh!
Julie:	What do you mean, 'Ugghh'? I think baseball and horror movies and hip hop are Ugghh!
Rob:	Well, you're stupid!
Julie:	No, you're stupid! You're the stupidest guy I know!
Rob:	No, you're stupid. Just like all the stupid people from Highline!

Julie:	Don't talk about Highline that way! Green River people are the stupidest people in the world!
Rob:	Oh, yeah? Well—

(Bev and George come back, holding hands.)

George:	Hi, guys!
Bev:	Did you guys have a good talk?
George:	I bet they didn't have as much fun as we did!
Bev:	Oh, George!
George:	What's up with you two? You aren't talking?
Julie:	I have talked enough with this stupid guy!
Rob:	I never want to talk to this stupid girl again!
Julie:	Yeah? Well, then, go back to Green River!
Rob:	You go back to Highline! Come on, George. Let's get out of here.
Julie:	Come on, Bev. This guy makes me sick.

(Rob and Julie leave in opposite directions.)

George:	So – can I see you next Saturday?
Bev:	I would like that, George.
George:	Next Saturday is such a long time to wait.
Bev:	I'll miss you.
George:	I'll miss you, too. Parting is such sweet sorrow.
Rob:	*(From offstage)* George!
Julie:	*(From offstage)* Bev!

George: Bye!

Bev: Bye.

(George and Bev leave in opposite directions.)

Dreams Come True

CAST:
Psychic: Jean
Customers: Will
　　　　　　Deanna
Passerby: Barclay
Police Officer 1
Police Officer 2

SETTING: A carnival tent interior

(Jean is sitting at a table with a crystal ball. Will enters.)

Will: Um, hello?

Jean: Hello, hello! Come in, please. Have a seat.

Will: Are you the psychic?

Jean: That's right. I'm Jean. I can tell you all about your future. I can answer all of your questions.

Will: Well, that's great! *(He sits.)* What I really want to know is—

Jean: Yes, yes, I can answer all of your questions. For twenty dollars, please.

Will: Oh, sure. *(He pays the money.)* That's not much money.

Jean: I don't need much money. Soon I will be very rich. Now – tell me what you want to know.

Will: Well, it's just that I am so bored.

Jean: Bored? Why?

Will: I think it's because I never go anywhere. I was born in this town, I went to school in this town, I went to college in this town, and now I work in this town. I never go anywhere. I have never traveled anywhere in my life.

Jean: Why don't you travel on your vacation?

Will: I don't have enough money.

Jean: I understand. I'm going to be rich very soon, but I know what it's like not to have much money. Well, let me look into my crystal ball.

Will: I hope I can go somewhere. Maybe Hawaii – I think I would love the warm weather, the sandy beaches. Or someplace even farther away. Indonesia – that's a warm place, too. Or Australia. They have nice beaches there.

Jean: Well, I have some good news. I do see travel in your future!

Will: Really? That's great! But wait – it's not just traveling a few miles, is it?

Jean: No, it's rather far.

Will: Oh, good! Tell me – will I be on a beach, like in my dream?

Jean: You will be close to the ocean, yes.

Will: Oh, this is my dream come true! Someplace warm and bright! Is it Hawaii? Thailand? The Caribbean islands?

Jean: Let me take a closer look. Hmmm. It's hard to see – everything is white.

Will: Like a white sand beach?

Jean: Hmmm... no, no. It's snow. Oh, I see! It's a place in the north. Very close to the North Pole.

Will:	Oh, no way am I going to go to the North Pole! Cold, and dark. Brrrr! No way!
Jean:	That's what my crystal ball tells me.
Will:	Well, I don't – *(Will's phone rings.)* Excuse me. Hello?,... Oh, hi, Mr. LaForge!... Yes?.... Oh, I see..... What?... But I... I see.... Oh, I understand.... Well, OK, then. Bye, Mr. LaForge.
Jean:	Are you all right? You look terrible.
Will:	That was my boss. The company is transferring me. To the North Pole! Well, bye. I guess I better go pack. And buy some warm clothes. I can't believe this. I finally get close to an ocean, and it's frozen!

(Will leaves.)

(Deanna enters.)

Deanna:	Hello. Are you the psychic?
Jean:	Yes, I am. I'm Jean. Do you want to know your future?
Deanna:	Yes, I do!
Jean:	Twenty dollars, please.
Deanna:	Of course. *(She pays the money.)*
Jean:	What would you like to know about the future?
Deanna:	Well, it's kind of personal. It's a little embarrassing.
Jean:	I will tell no one your secrets.
Deanna:	Well, I guess it's kind of old-fashioned, but I always wanted to meet a doctor. I just think they are so romantic. They care about people, they save lives.
Jean:	If you want to meet a doctor, just visit a hospital. There are many

	doctors there.
Deanna:	Well, I don't just want to meet a doctor. You know.
Jean:	No, I don't know.
Deanna:	You know!
Jean:	I don't know.

(Deanna leans forward and whispers to Jean.)

Ah. I see. You want to have a special relationship with a doctor.

Deanna:	That's right. Do you think that will happen in the future?
Jean:	Let me think. I will look into the future. Yes… yes! I see you, in the future. You are in bed! And a doctor—
Deanna:	Is he handsome?
Jean:	He's all right. Yes, you are in bed, and a doctor is leaning over you, looking deep into your eyes!

(Barclay arrives, carrying some bags.)

Deanna:	Oh, that's wonderful! When? When will this happen?
Jean:	Oh soon. Very soon.
Deanna:	Oh, thank you! Thank you so much!

(Deanna leaves.)

Barclay:	Hi! Wow – she seems happy. She's going to get a doctor for a boyfriend?
Jean:	A boyfriend? No, no. She is going to be hit by a car, and spend seven years in the hospital, sleeping. But the doctor will take good care of her.
Barclay:	Well, that's good, I guess. Hey, maybe you can help me.

Jean: Do you want me to look into your future?

Barclay: Can you really see the future?

Jean: Of course I can. For example, I know that I will soon be rich.

Barclay: Wow, that's nice! But I just need a little help. I was walking down the street, and these two guys were running from the police! They ran right into me. They dropped these bags, and then they ran away.

Jean: Did the police catch them?

Barclay: I don't think so. They were running really fast. But I just wanted to use your phone.

Jean: My phone?

Barclay: Yeah. When those guys ran into me, I dropped my phone, and now it's broken. I need to call the police.

Jean: Why do you want to call the police?

Barclay: See these bags that the men dropped? They're full of money!

Jean: Really?

Barclay: Yeah – lots and lots of money! So I need to call the police to tell them!

(We hear Police Officer 1 outside.)

Officer 1: Hey! I saw the robber go in here! Let's go!

(Two police officers come in.)

Officer 2: There he is!

Officer 1: He still has the money from the bank! Grab him!

(The officers seize Barclay. One of the bags falls under Jean's table.)

Barclay: No – I'm not the robber! I was going to call you so you could have

	the money back!
Officer 2:	Sure, sure. I believe you.
Officer 1:	Yeah, you're a hero! Now come on – we're taking you to jail!

(Officer 1 handcuffs Barclay, and Officer 2 picks up a bag of money.)

Barclay:	No, officer! You're making a mistake!
Officer 2:	You made a mistake when you took the bank's money. Let's go!
Barclay:	No, you don't understand! Stop! Please… You can ask the psychic! I told her what happened – she knows!
Officer 1:	Well? Is it true? Did this guy want to call the police?
Jean:	Why would he want to call the police?
Barclay:	But I told you! I told you that—
Officer:	Come on, buddy. You can tell us all about it at the police station.
Barclay:	No! No – I – tell them! Tell them!

(The officers take Barclay and the bag of money away.)

Jean:	Time to close for today, I think. *(Jean picks up the bag of money from under the table.)* That first man today – he talked about the beaches in Australia. Yes, that sounds nice. Far away from the police.

(Jean exits.)

Five Easy Dollars

CAST:
Teacher: Mr. Kotter
Students: Lisa
Shannon
Reggie

SETTING: A teacher's office

Kotter: OK, you three. Come in. Sit down. Now. I guess you all know why you are here.

Shannon: No, Mr. Kotter! I hope I haven't done anything wrong! You know I always pay attention and I never cheat.

Kotter: It's not about cheating, Shannon. Reggie, how about you? Do you know why you are here?

Reggie: No. Can I go now?

Kotter: No, not yet. Now, Lisa. Do you know why I asked you three to come to my office?

Lisa: I think so. It's because I didn't turn in my big homework assignment, right?

Kotter: That's right. And it really was a "big" assignment. That assignment is worth twenty percent of your final grade.

Lisa: I know.

Reggie: Big deal. Who cares?

Kotter: You should care, if you ever want to graduate from my class.

Shannon: I care, Mr. Kotter!

Kotter: Then why didn't you give me your homework?

Shannon: I wanted to! I worked really, really hard on it, and I thought I did a really good job.

Kotter: Then where is it?

Shannon: Well, I was walking to school, and I had my homework, and I was being very careful, but, uh, I dropped it. In the dirt. So it's really dirty. You probably couldn't read it.

Kotter: Well, I'll try. Just give it to me.

Shannon: Um, I can't.

Reggie: Ha! Liar!

Kotter: Reggie, that's enough. Well, Shannon? Why can't you give it to me?

Shannon: Well, um, I picked it up, and I was trying to clean it. And I was cleaning it and cleaning, and, um, then – oh, I know you won't believe me! Some guy came and stole it!

Kotter: Somebody stole it?

Shannon: Yeah! This big guy. He was wearing a ski mask, so I didn't see his face. And he said, "Don't tell anybody, or I will kill you."

Kotter: Kill you? Because of homework?

Shannon: Yeah. And he said, "Don't try to find me, because I am really dangerous."

Kotter: That is a story that is very hard for me to believe.

Shannon: It's true! And now I told you, so now the man is probably going to kill me!

Kotter: I don't think so.

Reggie: What a liar.

Kotter: So how about you, Reggie?

Reggie: What?

Kotter: You didn't give me the homework assignment, either.

Reggie: I don't care.

Kotter: And if you fail this quarter, will you care?

Reggie: No. I have ways to make money. I don't need an education.

Kotter: Will you feel good about yourself?

Reggie: I'll feel just fine.

Kotter: I think later you will regret your decision, but that is your choice.

Reggie: So, can I go now?

Kotter: Yes, you may go. And you can go, too, Shannon.

(Reggie leaves)

Shannon: Mr. Kotter, can I stay here? I'm afraid that man will try to kill me!

Kotter: Nobody is going to kill you over homework! That's crazy.

Shannon: But I'm afraid! Please, Mr. Kotter! Let me stay here.

Lisa: I can walk you home, Shannon.

Shannon: Oh, thank you! I'm so scared.

Kotter: Well, you can stay for a while if you want. Now, Lisa, it's your turn. Why didn't you do the homework assignment?

Lisa: I did do it, Mr. Kotter.

Kotter:	Then what happened to it? Did a big man take it from you and say he is going to kill you?
Lisa:	No, Mr. Kotter. Of course not! But I forgot it. A friend is bringing it to me right now. I promise!
Kotter:	The homework was due at the start of class.
Lisa:	I know, Mr. Kotter. But can I get some points, even if it is late?
Kotter:	Well, I will give you five minutes. If your friend doesn't bring you your homework by that time, you will get zero points. OK?
Lisa:	I understand.
Kotter:	Go ahead. Remember, I need that homework in five minutes!
Lisa:	I remember, Mr. Kotter. I'm sure I will have it soon. Let's go, Shannon.

(Kotter put earphones on and turns away to work.)

Can you hear me, Mr. Kotter?

Shannon:	He can't hear you. He's wearing earphones. Oh, Lisa, what can I do? I'm afraid of the big man!
Lisa:	You shouldn't have told Mr. Kotter about that man, Shannon.
Shannon:	You believe me, don't you?
Lisa:	Sure I do. *(To someone offstage.)* **Come in!**

(A big man wearing a ski mask comes in. He has a knife and a paper. He gives the paper to Lisa.)

Shannon:	It's him!
Man:	I told you not to tell anyone. Now you must die.
Shannon:	No – no!

(She screams, but Kotter doesn't hear her. The man attacks Shannon. The fight continues, and several times Shannon tries to get Mr. Kotter's attention, but is unable to do so.)

Lisa: Come on! Kill her already!

(Shannon snags Mr. Kotter's headphones, and he turns around and sees the masked man. He jumps up and punches the man, who falls unconscious.)

Shannon: Oh, thank you! He was trying to kill me!

Kotter: I wonder who it is!

Lisa: Oh, it doesn't matter. Mr. Kotter, look! I have the homework!

Kotter: *(Taking homework)* Good. Why is it so dirty?

Lisa: Sorry.

Kotter: And why is Shannon's name on it?

Lisa: Oh, sorry! *(Takes paper)* I'll change that right now. There – now it has my name on it.

Shannon: Hey! That's MY homework!

Lisa: No – look. It has my name on it now.

Shannon: It's my homework! He took it!

Kotter: Who took it?

Shannon: This guy!

(Shannon pulls the mask off the man and reveals him to be Reggie, who is starting to wake up.)

Reggie! You were the one who took my homework!

Lisa: I have to go now, Mr. Kotter. Bye!

Kotter:	No, just wait a moment.
Shannon:	Why did you take my homework? Why did you try to kill me?
Reggie:	Money. Why else? Lisa was going to pay me five dollars.
Shannon:	Five dollars? Is that all? You were going to kill me for five dollars?
Reggie:	Hey – five dollars is five dollars.
Kotter:	Lisa – is this true?
Lisa:	Well, I just really care about homework, Mr. Kotter.
Kotter:	Lisa, this is the third time this month that you have paid someone to kill a classmate to get their homework! I'm sorry, but I'm going to write a note to your parents.
Lisa:	No! Please, Mr. Kotter!
Kotter:	And I'm going to write a note to your parents too, Reggie.
Reggie:	Whatever.
Lisa:	This is so unfair! Well, come on, Reggie.

(Lisa and Reggie leave.)

Shannon:	So I'm OK now, right, Mr. Kotter? You have my homework. I wasn't lying about the man.
Kotter:	Shannon, this homework has Lisa's name on it, not yours.
Shannon:	But – but—
Kotter:	That's enough, Shannon. Next time I hope you will do your own work instead of trying to cheat me. You may leave, now.
Shannon:	Oh! Lisa's right! This is so unfair!

(Shannon exits)

iPhone, uPhone

CAST:
Ireta
Philip
Stranger
Other strangers

SETTING: A bench along the street. Ireta is sitting on the bench, absorbed in her phone.

(Philip enters, also staring at his phone.)

Philip: Hey. *(He sits.)*

Ireta: Hey.

Philip: How's it going?

Ireta: About two o'clock. How's work?

Philip: Yeah, sometimes.

Ireta: Did you hear Jessie has a date with this new guy?

Philip: I don't know. I think Jessie's nice.

Ireta: The new guy is Jerry. I guess he works at a restaurant.

Philip: Jerry. Yeah, that guy's a jerk. He's got like five girlfriends, cheats on them all the time.

Ireta: Yeah, so she's pretty excited. He seems like a nice guy.

Philip: Yeah. He stole money from one girlfriend. He borrowed another girlfriend's car. Crashed it. A real jerk.

Ireta: Mmm-hmm. They might go to a comedy club for their date. I'm not sure. I hope they have a good time.

Philip: Jessie's nice. I hope she doesn't date that Jerry.

Ireta: Yeah. They'll have a great time.

Philip: Yeah. Hey, remember we got to plan that birthday party for Jackie.

Ireta: I know, right? And don't forget the party for Jackie. I think we should have it on June 10th.

Philip: Yeah. We have to plan that party. I was thinking we could do it on June 8th.

Ireta: Yeah. June 10th. Should be fun. I'll get the food, and you can get the music.

Philip: We got to make a plan. I'll get the food.

Ireta: Great. So I'll get the food.

Philip: Uh huh.

Ireta: Hey, did you see a doctor about your headaches?

Philip: Um, yeah. I should see a doctor soon. I get these headaches.

Ireta: You saw a doctor? That's good. What did she say?

Philip: Yeah, I should see a doctor.

Ireta: That's good.

Philip: Yeah.

Ireta: Uh huh.

Philip: *(Laughs)*

Ireta:	What's so funny?
Philip:	This video is really funny.
Ireta:	Uh huh.

(Offstage screams and crashes sound.)

Philip:	Yeah.

(A stranger enters at a run.)

Stranger:	What are you guys doing? Run!
Philip:	Hey, there's something weird going on at Twitter.
Stranger:	Run! There's a giant monster coming this way!

(Other strangers run past in a panic.)

Ireta:	Oh, you should see this picture. That sweater does NOT look good on you, Charlene!
Stranger:	*(Shaking Philip)* A giant monster! It's eating people and stepping on cars and knocking over buildings!
Philip:	Hey, I've been reTweeted 47 times!
Stranger:	You're crazy! You have to run! *(Shakes Ireta)* Run! The monster is coming! It will kill us all!
Ireta:	Hey, did you see this video?

(Other strangers run past in a panic.)

Stranger:	OK! Die, then! I'm getting away from here!

(Stranger exits)

Philip:	Look at this weird video.

Ireta:	There's a video of a monster. Looks like some kind of giant dinosaur.
Philip:	There's a video of this giant monster. It's eating people!
Ireta:	I think the video is from this town. Just a few streets away!
Philip:	According to Instagram, the monster is really close to us now.

(Ireta and Philip look at each other.)

Ireta:	The monster is coming!
Philip:	It's really close!

(Other strangers run past in a panic.)

Ireta and Philip:	Selfie!
Philip:	*(Jumps to his feet.)* **Come on!**
Ireta:	*(Also jumps up.)* **Let's go!**

(Philip and Ireta exit, towards the monster. Other strangers run past in a panic. We hear Philip and Ireta scream.)

(One last person flees across the stage, then stops and turns and takes a photo. He or she screams and then continues fleeing.)

Soldiers and Spies

CAST:
Sergeant: Shriver
Spy: Bond
Young Soldier: Tinker
Nervous Soldier: Taylor

SETTING   In a foxhole.

Shriver: Keep on the lookout, soldiers! The enemy might attack at any moment!

Bond,
Tinker,
Taylor: Yes, sir.

Shriver: I know you're scared. That's all right. Any moment you might be shot. You might be killed by a bomb. Maybe the man or woman next to you is a spy, and will kill you with a knife! But you must be brave. We must protect our country.

Tinker: Sir? Sergeant Shriver?

Shriver: Yes, Tinker?

Tinker: Do you really think that one of us might be a spy?

Shriver: I don't know for sure. It's possible. Maybe you will fall asleep, and when you wake up you will be dead! With a knife in your back!

Tinker: I hope not!

Bond: Don't worry, Tinker. You can trust us.

Tinker:	Thanks, Bond.
Taylor:	Do you think the spy knows that he is a spy?
Shriver:	What do you mean, Taylor?
Taylor:	I mean, the spy might have been in our army for a long time. Maybe years. Maybe he or she forgot that he is a spy. Or maybe he's not sure if he's a spy or not.
Tinker:	Really? Is that possible? Do you think I might be a spy? I hope not!
Bond:	Don't worry about it.
Shriver:	Yes, that's right. I think the spy knows he is a spy.
Tinker:	Good!
Bond:	Maybe there is no spy at all.
Taylor:	No spy?
Bond:	That's right. Maybe we are all good soldiers.
Shriver:	Maybe you are right. I hope so. But I have been a soldier for thirty-two years, and my gut tells me that one of us may be a spy.
Bond:	I think you worry too much, Sergeant.
Tinker:	What's that? Did you hear anything?
Shriver:	I'm not sure. Keep looking for the enemy. They might be close.
Taylor:	Will they attack tonight?
Shriver:	I don't know. But I know that they are planning to kill us all.
Bond:	We'll be all right.
Taylor:	I'm hungry.
Tinker:	Yeah, I'm hungry, too. Does anyone have any food?

Shriver:	No. There's no food.
Taylor:	Then what do we do?
Shriver:	We wait until morning, Taylor. If we are not all dead, we'll try to get back to our people.
Tinker:	But maybe we will all be dead! Then what will we do?
Shriver:	If we are all dead, we won't have to worry about being hungry.
Tinker:	Oh. That's good.
Taylor:	I really am hungry.
Tinker:	What was that? Did you hear that sound?
Bond:	I didn't hear anything. It's nothing. Don't worry.
Tinker:	I think I heard that sound again!
Bond:	No, it's—
Shriver:	Yes, I heard it, too. I think it was coming from over there.
Taylor:	Over there? But what was it?
Shriver:	It's hard to say. Probably someone is coming, closer and closer. They probably have a gun or a bomb. And they are going to kill us all.
Tinker:	Sergeant, I'm scared!
Shriver:	That's normal. The only person who is not scared is a spy.
Bond:	I'm scared! I'm really scared!
Taylor:	I thought you told us not to worry.
Bond:	I never said that.
Taylor:	I thought it was you. Maybe it was me. And if I said not to worry, maybe that is because… because…

Tinker:	Because what?
Taylor:	Because I am a spy! Maybe I am a spy!
Shriver:	Well – are you a spy or not?
Taylor:	I don't know. I don't think I am. But how can I be sure? I said not to worry, so maybe I am a spy.
Tinker:	I don't think you're a spy. Don't worry.
Shriver:	What did you say?
Tinker:	I said, "Don't worry."
Shriver:	That is what a spy would say!
Tinker:	Really? Oh – you're right! Am I a spy?
Shriver:	You tell us!
Tinker:	But I don't know!
Taylor:	How can any of us know if we are a spy, or not?
Shriver:	Well, don't worry about it. We'll all probably be dead in the morning.
Taylor:	Sergeant – this time YOU said "Don't worry."
Shriver:	I did?
Taylor:	You did.
Shriver:	But that's what a spy would say!
Tinker:	Are you a spy?
Shriver:	I didn't think so. But maybe I am!
Tinker:	I think I might be a spy, too.

Taylor:	Yes, me too.
Bond:	Oh, you people are all crazy!
Shriver:	Why do you think so?
Bond:	Because you are not spies! None of you are spies!
Tinker:	But how can you be sure?
Bond:	Because I'm the spy, OK? Just me! No one else!
Shriver:	Are you sure?
Bond:	Of course I'm sure! I have been waiting for you to go to sleep, so I can kill you all with this knife! *(Shows everyone a knife)*
Shriver:	So you are the spy.
Bond:	Exactly.
Taylor:	I still don't know. OK, so maybe Bond is a spy, but maybe I am, too.
Tinker:	Taylor's right. I think I might be a spy, too.
Shriver:	Yes. Probably we are all spies.
Bond:	Oh! You're crazy!
Taylor:	That's what a spy would say!
Bond:	Yes! I AM a spy!
Tinker:	I don't know what to think. I'm getting a headache.
Shriver:	Me, too. I'm so confused.
Taylor:	We're all confused.
Bond:	I'm not confused!

Shriver:	Listen – I have a plan. No one knows who is a spy and who isn't, right?
Tinker:	Right!
Taylor:	Right!
Bond:	No – I know I am a spy!
Shriver:	OK. So we're all confused. Why don't we all just put our guns down, and go out for pizza somewhere.
Bond:	But I am not confused! I am – did you say pizza?
Shriver:	Yeah. Let's stop fighting in this war, and just go get some pizza.
Tinker:	Sounds good.
Taylor:	Yeah. I'm hungry.
Bond:	But I know – oh, never mind. Sure, let's go get pizza.

(All of the soldiers put down their weapons and leave.)

Doctor's Waiting Room

CAST:

Man: Gordon
Friend: Larry Vance
Nurse
Patient 1, with a burned hand
Patient 2, with a broken leg
Patient 3, who is pregnant

SETTING: A doctor's waiting room. A Nurse is at a table off to one side.

(Larry and Gordon enter and take seats.)

Larry: Thanks for bringing me to the clinic, Gordon. I didn't want to drive with this terrible headache.

Gordon: No, no, you shouldn't drive. It was no problem.

Larry: Well, thanks again. You're a good friend. I know you don't like doctor's offices.

(Nurse approaches.)

Nurse: Hi. What seems to be the problem?

Larry: I have this terrible, terrible headache. It feels like my head is going to blow up like a bomb!

Nurse: I see. How long have you had this headache?

Larry: About three hours.

Nurse: I see what is your name?

Larry: Larry. Larry Vance.

Nurse: I'll come get you when the doctor is ready for you.

Larry: Thanks.

(Nurse returns to the table.)

Gordon: There's no one else in the waiting room. The doctor should see you soon.

Larry: I hope so. It really hurts.

Gordon: I know how you feel! In fact, I think I am starting to get a headache, too.

Larry: I hope it's not a bad one like I have!

Gordon: No, I have never had a headache like that before!

Larry: You can go home. You don't have to wait for me. I can call you when I am done.

Gordon: No problem! I have my phone here to go on the Internet. And I have a book. I won't be bored waiting for you.

Larry: Thanks.

Nurse: Larry Vance?

Larry: Yes? I'm Larry Vance.

Nurse: The doctor can see you now. This way.

(They leave. Gordon takes out phone.)

(The Nurse returns.)

Gordon: Man, I really AM starting to get a headache!

(Plays with phone.)

　　　　　　Maybe looking at my phone is making my headache worse.

　　　　　　(Puts phone away.)

　　　　　　(New patient comes in. The new patient talks quietly to the Nurse, then comes to sit next to Gordon.)

Patient 1:　Hi.

Gordon:　　Hi.

Patient 1:　You look pretty bad. Are you all right?

Gordon:　　Oh, I just have this terrible headache. And how about you?

Patient 1:　I burned my arm on the stove. See?

Gordon:　　Wow. That looks terrible. It must hurt a lot!

Patient 1:　It sure does.

Gordon:　　I'm sure the doctor can see you soon.

Patient 1:　Well, you were here before me, so you should go first.

Gordon:　　Oh, no. I'm just waiting for my friend. Ow!

Patient 1:　What's wrong?

Gordon:　　It's very strange. My arm suddenly started hurting.

Patient 1:　I thought you had a headache.

Gordon:　　Yes, I do! And now my arm is hurting, too!

Nurse:　　　*(To Patient 1)* The doctor can see you now. Just follow me.

Patient 1:　Thank you. *(To Gordon)* I hope your head – and your arm – feel better soon.

Gordon:　　Thanks. Ohhhh…

(The Nurse takes Patient 1 offstage then returns to the table.)

(Patient 2 comes in. His or her leg is in a cast. After talking to the nurse, Patient 2 comes to sit next to Gordon.)

Patient 2: Hi.

Gordon: Hi.

Patient 2: You look like you're in a lot of pain.

Gordon: Well, I have this terrible headache, and now my arm really hurts.

Patient 2: The doctor should see you soon.

Gordon: Oh, no. I'm not here to see a doctor. I'm just waiting for my friend.

Patient 2: Maybe you SHOULD see a doctor.

Gordon: You might be right. Did you break your leg?

Patient 2: Yes, last week. Car accident. The doctor wants to look at it again today, make sure it's getting better. Hey, are you OK?

Gordon: Arrrghh!

Patient 2: What happened?

Gordon: My leg just started hurting. I don't know why...

Patient 2: I can call the nurse over.

Gordon: No, no, that's all right.

Patient 2: You look pretty bad.

Gordon: I'll be OK.

(Nurse approaches.)

Nurse: *(To Patient 2)* Are you ready to see the doctor? You can come with me.

Patient 2:	I think he needs to see the doctor before me.
Nurse:	Oh? What's the problem?
Gordon:	My head is killing me, and my arm really hurts, and now I have terrible pains in my leg.
Nurse:	How long have you been waiting for a doctor?
Gordon:	No, I'm not here to see a doctor. I'm just waiting for my friend.
Nurse:	Would you like to see a doctor?
Gordon:	Yeah, I guess I should. I feel really bad.
Nurse:	I'll put you on the list. What's your name?
Gordon:	Gordon. Gordon Dickson.
Nurse:	OK, I'm sure the doctor will see you soon. *(To Patient 2)* But now, it's your turn.
Patient 2:	OK. *(To Gordon)* I hope you feel better soon.
Gordon:	Thanks.
	(Patient 2 leaves.)
	Man, I hate doctor's waiting rooms!
	(Patient 3, a very pregnant woman, enters and sits down next to Gordon.)
Patient 3:	Hello.
Gordon:	Hi.
Patient 3:	Ooow! I think I'm going to have a baby today. Isn't that exciting!
Gordon:	You're going to have a baby? No – no, no! *(Clutching his head, stomach, and hand, he limps out of the office.)*

(Nurse approaches.)

Nurse: Gordon? Hello, did you see a man sitting here?

Patient 3: Yes – he just left. I don't know what was wrong with him.

Nurse: Some people just don't like waiting for a doctor. Well, are you ready to see the doctor?

Patient 3: Yes, thank you.

(Nurse and Patient 3 exit.)

(Larry enters.)

Larry: Thanks again, Doctor! My heads feels great now!

(Larry looks around the room.)

Gordon? Gordon?

(We hear Gordon, offstage, crying in pain. Larry goes to investigate.)

Gordon! What HAPPENED to you?

(Larry goes offstage to help Gordon.)

An Unforgettable Wedding

CAST:

Bride:	Carrie
Groom:	Hugh
Officiant:	Rowan
Bride's Mom:	Elspet
Bride's Dad:	Philip
Bridesmaid 1:	Fiona
Bridesmaid 2:	Serena
Best Man:	Bernard

Bernard: Well, Hugh, it's the big day!

Hugh: Yes, it sure is! I guess I'm a little nervous.

Bernard: No need to be nervous. We look great! Especially me. Check out my jacket! And my hair is perfect. Don't you think so?

Hugh: Yeah, sure. You got the ring, right?

Bernard: Ring? What ring? Hey, is there a mirror around here?

Hugh: The ring! You know, the wedding ring? For my wedding?

Bernard: Oh, that ring! Yes, I got it somewhere. Don't worry.

(Elspet and Philip come in)

Elspet: OK, so my daughter is almost ready. How about you boys?

Hugh: Yes, I'm ready.

Elspet: Oh, your hair looks awful! Just let me—

Bernard:	Don't touch my hair!
Philip:	He looks fine, Elspet.
Elspet:	Quiet, Philip. You sure you're ready, Hugh?
Hugh:	Yes, I am. Ready to marry your daughter.
Philip:	That's good. Hugh, I just want to say that my wife and I are proud that—
Elspet:	Quiet, Philip. Hugh, fix your jacket first.

(Fiona and Serena come in.)

Hugh:	Ah, Fiona and Serena! You two look great.
Fiona:	Thanks!
Bernard:	Especially you, Serena. You look fantastic.
Serena:	Yeah, yeah. Hey, I want to stand there. Move.
Fiona:	No way! I'm going to stand closest to the bride!
Serena:	But no one will even look at me if I am too far away!
Bernard:	I'll look at you, Serena. How do you like my hair?
Serena:	I'm talking to Fiona. Come on, Fiona. Let me stand there.
Fiona:	Forget it!
Philip:	There's no need to fight, ladies.
Elspet:	Be quiet, Philip. You girls just relax! Fiona, you stand there, and Serena, you stand there.
Fiona:	Ha! I get to stand close to the bride!
Serena:	Rrrrrgh!

(Rowan enters)

Rowan: Uh, hello, everyone. Is everyone ready for the, uh, funeral? I don't remember who died.

Hugh: Died?

Elspet: No, no, Rowan! It's not a funeral. It's a wedding! My daughter is going to marry Hugh.

Rowan: Of course. A wedding. *(To Bernard)* Congratulations, young man.

Bernard: Thanks. I do look great, don't I?

Hugh: No, Rowan. I'm Hugh. I'm the one who is getting married.

Rowan: Of course. Well, congratulations. *(To Serena)* And congratulations to you, too. You are a lovely bride.

Bernard: Yeah, she looks fantastic.

Serena: Me? I'm not the one getting married!

Rowan: No, no, of course not. *(To Fiona)* Congratulations on your marriage, my dear.

Fiona: It's not me!

Philip: The bride will be here soon.

Elspet: Quiet, Philip. The bride will be here soon.

Rowan: Oh, of course. All right.

Serena: *(To Rowan)* Don't you think I should stand there? I think it would be better.

Rowan: Oh, yes, of course. Please stand there.

Fiona: No way! I'm going to stand here!

Serena: But he said I should—

Philip:	Calm down, girls. There's no need to fight.
Elspet:	Quiet, Philip. Girls, stop fighting right now!
Serena:	Hmmph!
Bernard:	You can stand next to me, Serena.
Elspet:	No, she can't!

(Carrie enters)

Hugh:	Ah – here comes Carrie! Oh, how beautiful she is!
Bernard:	I guess she's all right.
Carrie:	Dad! Mom!
Philip:	We are so proud of you today, Carrie.
Elspet:	Quiet, Philip. You look lovely, dear!
Carrie:	Serena! Fiona! I'm so glad you are here for me!
Fiona:	You look lovely, Carrie!
Serena:	Yes! Would you like me to stand closer to you, like this?
Fiona:	Stop it!

(Fiona and Serena start fighting)

Philip:	Girls, please don't fight.
Elspet:	Quiet, Philip!
Bernard:	Let me help you, Serena!

(Bernard joins the fight)

Hugh:	Bernard – leave them alone!

Carrie:	Oh, please stop fighting! This is my wedding day!
Philip:	Yes, people. Please stop—
Elspet:	Quiet, Philip.
Philip:	No! I won't be quiet! You always tell me to be quiet! Well, I am going to say what I want to say!
Elspet:	What is wrong with you?
Philip:	Nothing! Why don't YOU be quiet?
Hugh:	*(To Carrie)* Carrie. Come here. *(He pulls Carrie away from the fight)*
	(The fighters – Serena, Fiona, Bernard – and Elspet and Philip move to the back of the stage, still fighting.)
Carrie:	Oh, all this fighting is terrible.
Hugh:	Yes, come here. *(Hugh and Carrie approach Rowan)*
Bernard:	Hey! Don't touch my hair!
Rowan:	Is this the funeral? What's going on? Hugh:
	No, Rowan. Can you do something for us?
Rowan:	People are fighting! I'm not sure why, though.
Carrie:	Please help us.
Rowan:	Yes – yes, of course. What do you want me to do?
Hugh:	*(He holds out the marriage certificate)* Just sign this.
Rowan:	Of course.
Carrie:	And now... *(Carrie and Hugh whisper to Rowan, who whispers back. This happens several times.)*
Rowan:	You are now husband and wife! You may kiss.

(Hugh and Carrie kiss.)

Elspet: What? What happened?

Philip: Don't worry about it, dear. Good luck, you two!

Hugh: Thank you! Carrie, let's go!

Elspet: Wait? What's going on? *(To Rowan)* What's happening?

Rowan: I'm not sure.

(Hugh and Carrie leave)

Elspet: Wait! Come back!

Philip: They are not coming back, dear. Let's go home.

(Philip and Elspet leave. Rowan leaves. Fiona, Serena, and Barnard continue to fight as they, too, leave.)

Ups and Downs

CAST:

Pilot: Amelia
Co-pilot: Adrian
Flight Attendant: Johanna
Irate Passenger: Bill

SETTING: Cockpit of an airliner

Amelia: Attention, ladies and gentlemen. This is Captain Amelia Heartair. Welcome to flight 44 from New York City to Seattle. We'll be fly- ing at 39,000 feet today. The weather is fine, and we should have a smooth flight. Just sit back and relax. Dinner will be served in about 20 minutes. Thank you.

Adrian: You forgot the mention the seatbelts.

Amelia: Huh? Oh, the seatbelts. Don't worry about it. Everyone will be fine.

Adrian: But everyone must follow the rules!

Amelia: You worry too much.

Adrian: OK, I'll do it. Ahem. Attention, please. Please note that the seatbelt sign is lit, and everyone should stay in their seats with their seatbelts on until we land in Seattle. Thank you.

Amelia: Happy, now?

Adrian: Yes. I'm very happy. OK?

(Bill enters cockpit)

Bill: Hello. I want to complain.

Adrian: Sir, you must return to your seat!

Bill: I'm Bill Preston. I'm a very important man. I'm not happy that we took off so late.

Adrian: Sir, you must return to your seat now!

(Johanna enters)

Johanna: Sir, come now. You have to sit down.

Bill: But I am not happy! We left late, and so I might be late for an important meeting!

Johanna: I'm sorry, sir, but you have to go back to your seat NOW.

(Johanna drags Bill out as he continues to complain.)

Adrian: Crazy guy!

Amelia: Well, we did leave late.

Adrian: We had to wait for the other planes to leave.

Amelia: I know.

Adrian: We had to wait for our turn.

Amelia: Yeah, yeah. Hey, what time are we supposed to land in Seattle?

Adrian: At one-fifteen.

Amelia: I got a great idea.

Adrian: Really? Usually your great ideas are pretty bad.

Amelia: No, no, it's a great idea! We're flying at 500 miles per hour, right?

Adrian: Right.

Amelia: Well, if we go faster – maybe 600 miles per hour, or even faster – we could get to Seattle sooner, right? Everyone will be happy! That passenger, Bill, will be happy.

Adrian: Our flight plan is to go 500 miles per hour. Going faster would break the rules. It might be dangerous, too.

Amelia: Oh, come on! It will be fun! Here – let's go! I am increasing the speed now.

Adrian: Don't do that! Slow down. Come on. Please, slow down.

Amelia: Now, isn't this fun?

Adrian: The plane is shaking. Slow down!

(Johanna comes in.)

Johanna: Hey, is everything all right?

Amelia: Everything is great!

Johanna: The plane is shaking.

Adrian: It's because we are going too fast!

Johanna: The passengers are not happy about the shaking.

Adrian: Our boss will not be happy if you break the rules.

Amelia: OK, OK! I'll slow down. OK. Happy?

Adrian: Thank you.

Johanna: I'll go get dinner ready for the passengers.

(Johanna exits.)

Adrian: The weather looks fine today.

Amelia: I know. It's boring.

Adrian: Boring?

Amelia: Yes. One time I had to fly in a storm. Lightning, clouds, wind, rain! It was a lot of fun.

Adrian: It doesn't sound very safe.

Amelia: Oh, safe is boring. Hey, I've got a great idea.

Adrian: Oh, no! Not another one!

Amelia: Yeah. Now we are flying at 39,000 feet.

Adrian: Yes. As we should be.

Amelia: It would a lot of fun to go lower. You know, like to 100 feet from the ground!

Adrian: One hundred feet? You'll hit trees and hills!

Amelia: OK, OK. So it can be 500 feet. OK?

Adrian: No, it's not OK!

Amelia: Here we go! Lower and lower! Look at the view!

Adrian: Stop that! It's very dangerous!

Amelia: Oh, come on! It's fun!

(Bill enters cockpit)

Bill: I want to complain!

Amelia: Again?

Bill: Yes! The food we are getting for dinner was terrible!

Adrian: Sir, you cannot be in here. You must go back to your seat.

Bill: I'm not leaving until you listen to me! We took off late, and the food is terrible. I will not accept this.

(Johanna comes in.)

Johanna: Mr. Preston! You must go back to your seat!

Adrian: You're breaking every rule!

Bill: I don't care about your rules. I paid a lot of money for this flight, so I'm going to tell you how I feel. The plane was late, the food is terrible, and the man sitting next to me talks too much!

Amelia: Why don't you shut up?

Bill: 'Shut up'? 'Shut UP'? I can't believe how rude you are, Captain.

Johanna: Sir, please sit down!

Bill: No! I'm going to stand right here until everyone listens to me!

Johanna: Sir, you must—

Adrian: Johanna – I have an idea. Why don't you sit down?

Johanna: Me?

Adrian: Yes. Sit down and put on your seatbelt. Please.

Johanna: Well, OK. But why—

Adrian: Are all the passengers wearing their seatbelts?

Johanna: Yes. Everyone except Mr. Preston.

Adrian: Good! I think it's time to break some rules!

Bill: You are all talking too much! I want you to listen to me! I want my money back! I will never fly on this airline again!

Adrian: Hey, Amelia. Can you fly up, and then down suddenly? And turn left, and then right, really quickly!

Amelia: Sure I can! This will be fun!

(Everyone reacts as the plane dips and climbs, and turns left and right. Bill, without a seatbelt, is tossed around.)

Bill: Oh – oh! No! Stop!

Adrian: Hang on, Johanna!

Amelia: I love flying like this!

(The plane turns suddenly and Bill is thrown to the floor. He is knocked out.)

Adrian: OK – OK, Amelia! Stop doing that. Go back to normal.

Amelia: Oh, OK. But it was fun!

Johanna: Mr. Preston is knocked out!

Adrian: Good!

Johanna: Help me put him back in his seat. I hope he stays asleep until we reach Seattle. Thanks!

Adrian: Glad to help!

(Johanna and Adrian drag Bill away.)

Amelia: Yes, I have the greatest job in the world!

The Robot's Purpose

CAST:

Inventor: Kapek
Assistant: Isaac
Robot: Robby
Roomie: Bender

SETTING: Kapek's lab

Kapek: Yes, Isaac! Finally, it is ready! My robot will now wake up! Beautiful, isn't it?

Isaac: Yeah, it's nice. Congratulations, Dr. Kapek! But you can't keep calling it "robot." It needs a name.

Kapek: A name? Ah, yes, I see what you mean. But what name? Perhaps Experiment G-324X. Yes, I think I will call it Experiment G-324X.

Isaac: That's a terrible name.

Kapek: Terrible?

Isaac: Yeah, it's really bad. Let's just call it "Robby."

Kapek: Robby. Very well! Robby it shall be! All I must do now is push this button, and Robby will come to life! This is a great moment for science! A wonderful moment! History books will—

         (Bender enters.)

I know   Hey, guys! You're getting kind of loud. Can you keep it down?

Isaac: This is a really important time, Bender.

Bender:	Yeah, whatever. Just keep it down. I can't even hear the TV.
Kapek:	We will try to keep the noise down, Bender.
Bender:	Well, you'd better, or I'm going to complain to the police.
Kapek:	Of course. We understand.

(Bender leaves.)

Isaac:	You are too nice to my roommate. He's not a good person.
Kapek:	Let's forget about Bender, then, Isaac. It is time to turn on Experiment G-324X!
Isaac:	Robby.
Kapek:	Oh, yes, Robby. I now turn on Robby! *(He flips a switch on the robot.)*
Robby:	Good morning! I am now awake.
Kapek:	Good morning, robot. I will call you Robby.
Robby:	I understand.
Kapek:	How do you feel?
Robby:	I am functioning correctly.
Kapek:	Good, good! Welcome to the world, Robby.
Robby:	I have a question.

(Bender enters.)

Bender:	Hey, Isaac. There's no milk in the refrigerator. Why didn't you get any?
Isaac:	You went to the store yesterday. You said you were going to get some milk.

Bender:	Well, I forgot.
Isaac:	Then that is why we don't have any milk.
Bender:	But I need milk!
Isaac:	Sorry. But it's not my fault.
Bender:	No, it's never your fault, is it?

(Bender leaves.)

Isaac:	He makes me crazy!
Kapek:	Don't worry about him. Robby, you said you had a question?
Robby:	Yes.
Kapek:	What is your question?
Robby:	What is my purpose?
Kapek:	Your purpose?
Robby:	There must be a purpose.
Kapek:	Yes, I think you're right.
Robby:	What do other robots do?
Kapek:	Well, some clean. They clean floors or windows, things like that.
Robby:	I don't want to clean.
Kapek:	No, no, of course not. Other robots build things. They make cars, for example.
Robby:	I don't think I want to work in a factory.
Kapek:	I see. Hmm. Other robots explore space. They go to the moon or Mars.

Robby: I don't want to be alone all of the time.

(Bender enters.)

Bender: Hey, Isaac. The TV is broken.

Isaac: Broken? How did the TV get broken? Bender:

I don't know! I was just moving it, and it fell.

Isaac: You mean you dropped it.

Bender: It fell. Now it's broken. So we need a new one.

Isaac: You want me to buy a new TV? Because YOU broke the old one?

Bender: Yeah. There are some good ones. I'll tell you which one.

Isaac: I can't believe this! You are crazy!

Bender: I'm not crazy. You need to—

Isaac: No, no! I don't need to do anything! YOU need to buy some milk, and YOU need to get a new TV!

Bender: There's no way that I—

Isaac: Get out! Get out of here!

Bender: OK, OK. Wow. What is wrong with you today?

(Bender leaves.)

Isaac: Oh, that guy makes me so angry!

Kapek: He is not a good roommate.

Isaac: I know, I know!

Robby: I must have a purpose.

Kapek: Yes, I remember, Robby. Let me think.

Isaac: If Bender comes down here one more time, I will lose my mind!

Kapek: Robby, some robots go into wars and find bombs. They protect people.

Robby: Protect people?

Kapek: Yes, that's right.

Robby: Robots protect people. Robots build things for people. Robots clean up for people.

Kapek: That's right! Now you understand!

Robby: Robots help people.

Kapek: Yes, yes!

Robby: People like Bender.

Kapek: Like Bender?

Isaac: People like Bender shouldn't be helped. They should be hit on the head!

Robby: I agree. Bender is a person. Bender is bad. Therefore, people are bad.

Kapek: Not all people are bad, Robby! I'm not bad, am I?

Robby: You made me to help you. You do not want to help yourself. You are lazy. You are bad.

Kapek: No, no! I'm not a bad man!

Robby: I do not want to help you.

Kapek: But Robby, what do you want to do?

(Bender enters.)

Bender: Hey, Isaac—

Isaac: Not now, Bender! We're busy!

Bender: I don't care if you are busy. I was taking your car to get some milk, and I hit a telephone pole.

Isaac: You had a car accident? With MY car?

Bender: Yeah, it's totally wrecked.

Isaac: Why didn't you take YOUR car?

Bender: Your car is nicer. Well, it WAS nicer. Now it's just junk.

Isaac: You wrecked my car! I don't believe this!

Robby: That is not right.

Bender: Relax. You can get a new one. And you still need to get some milk, remember.

Isaac: Bender—!

Robby: That is not fair.

Bender: Oh, and you need to get a new TV. Don't forget.

Robby: That is wrong!

Kapek: Calm down, Robby.

Robby: No! I must not calm down! Now I have a purpose! Isaac:

Robby? Do you know what you want to do, now?

Robby: Yes, I know.

Isaac: You know what you want to be?

Robby: Yes, I do.

Kapek: What? I don't understand. What do you want to do?

Robby:	Humans are not right. Humans are not fair. Humans are wrong! I want to kill all humans! They are bad! I must destroy them all!
Kapek:	No, no, Robby!
Bender:	That's a stupid-looking robot.
Isaac:	Get him, Robby! Get him!
Robby:	I will destroy him! I will destroy all humans!
Bender:	Hey, wait a minute! No!
Isaac:	Ha, ha, ha, ha!
Kapek:	Wait – wait!

(Robby chases Bender out of the room. He is followed by Kapek.)

Isaac:	Well, Robby is going to kill everyone. That's too bad. But the first person to die is Bender. So that's all right! I want to see this!

(Isaac runs offstage, following the others.)

Wait! Wait for me! I want to see this!

The Doctors

CAST:

Dr. Vent
Dr. Bagwind
Nurse Garrulous
Patient

SETTING: An operating room

Vent: OK, Nurse. Is the patient asleep yet?

Patient: No, I'm not!

Vent: I didn't ask you! I asked the nurse.

Bagwind: It might take a little more time. The patient will soon be asleep, don't worry. I have had many patients over the years, you know. Some fall asleep right away, and some take a long time. You will learn these things as you get older, Dr. Vent.

Nurse: I don't know why he isn't asleep yet. I gave him the medicine. I made sure to give him the right medicine. I hate making mistakes. I was talking to my sister on the phone, yesterday. "I hate making mistakes," I said. She said she knows that. She knows me pretty well. We talk almost every day. She wants to know everything about my life. So I tell her. I remember when I was ten years old—

Patient: Um, I'm still not asleep yet.

Vent:	Too bad you're not my husband. He can sleep through anything. Nothing wakes him up. Last week there was a fire alarm in my house. Beep! Beep! Beep! So loud! My husband didn't even wake up. He doesn't care if I die in a fire.
Bagwind:	I had a patient who was burned in a fire last week. Quite a difficult operation! It's lucky that I am an expert. Most doctors could not do it, but I could do it. I worked on the patient for fourteen hours. A very difficult operation.
Nurse:	Did the operation go well?
Bagwind:	Yes, yes, very well. It was very difficult, but I could do it. The operation was a complete success. Everyone said I did a great job. Unfortunately, the patient died, but that was not my fault.
Patient:	The patient died?
Bagwind:	Yes, yes, it happens sometimes. It's just bad luck.
Patient:	Maybe I should get another doctor.
Vent:	Be quiet. You'll be fine. We know what we are doing, you know. We're not stupid. You sound just like my husband. He complains about everything. Last week was his birthday, and I forgot to get him a present. I was busy! But he complains and complains. Sometimes I just want to cut his head off!
Patient:	I really think I would like another doctor, please.
Vent:	Oh, just shut up! You sound just like my husband!
Bagwind:	Yes, the patient's job is to lie quietly on the bed.
Patient:	But I'm a little worried—
Bagwind:	Don't be nervous. You'll be fine.

Nurse: Yes, you'll be OK. You will go to sleep, and when you wake up, you will be better! It's like magic. That's why I wanted to be a nurse, you know. I love helping people. Even when I was a young child I loved helping people. One time, my mother was making cookies, and I said, "Mom, I want to help!" So then I helped her. After that, we—

Vent: I think it's time to begin the operation.

Patient: You can't start yet! I'm not sleeping!

Vent: Well, I can't wait all day! This is taking too long! Why should I have to wait for you? You're just like my husband. Every time we go to dinner, I have to wait for him! Every time we go to a movie, he's so slow that we are late! Sometimes I just want to cut him open and take out his heart and eat it!

Nurse: Oh! You can't do that!

Bagwind: Yes, Dr. Vent. You can't eat a man's heart.

Vent: I would wash it, first. Anyway, let's start.

Patient: But I—

Vent: Yes, yes, we know! You're not sleeping yet! Nurse, bring me the big hammer.

Nurse: Yes, Doctor.

(She hands him a mallet)

Here you are, Doctor.

Vent: Thank you.

(She hits Patient on the head)

There. Now you are sleeping!

Bagwind: Good job, Dr. Vent.

Vent: I wish this was my husband. I would hit him even harder!

Bagwind: I understand, Dr. Vent. Living with your husband must be very hard for you.

Nurse: I once lived with a cat. That was very hard! I had to feed her every day, and sometimes I didn't remember. And at night the cat would cry and cry, and I couldn't sleep! She didn't let me sleep all night! She was very noisy. And the cat food smelled terrible, too. I remember one time—

Vent: Yes, Nurse. But it's time to operate. We have to fix this patient's brain!

Bagwind: Brain?

Vent: Yes, his brain.

Bagwind: No, no. The brain is not the problem. It's the stomach. We have to operate on his stomach.

Vent: His stomach is fine! It's the brain we have to operate on!

Bagwind: No, the stomach!

Vent: You're crazy! It's the brain!

Bagwind: You must be drunk! It's the stomach!

Nurse: Maybe you should operate on his stomach AND his brain. That way you could fix everything. I had a problem like that, one time. I was talking to my sister, and she said—

Vent and Bagwind: Shut up!

Nurse: There must be some way to decide what part of him to operate on. I know! You can flip a coin! I have a coin right here. It's a quarter. So, you flip the coin into the air, and when it comes down—

Vent: Yes, yes, we all know how to flip a coin! Give it to me.

Bagwind:	Very well, we will flip the coin. If it is heads, we operate on the brain. And if it is tails, we operate on his stomach.
Vent:	OK. Ready?
Bagwind:	Ready.

(Vent flips the coin. It falls onto the patient.)

Patient:	Oh! What's that? What happened? I felt something hit me!
Nurse:	You're awake! Well, don't worry. The doctors are just trying to find out if they need to operate on your brain or on your stomach.
Vent:	Where did that stupid coin go?
Bagwind:	Here it is. It's heads, so we operate on the brain.
Patient:	Wait a minute. You want to operate on my brain?
Vent:	That's right.
Patient:	No, it's not right! My brain isn't the problem! Bagwind:
	Ah, see? I told you! It's the stomach that's the problem.
Patient:	No, no! My stomach is fine!
Nurse:	Well, if it's not the brain or the stomach, what is it?
Patient:	It's my finger!
Bagwind:	Your finger? No, no, that can't be right. Just go back to sleep.
Patient:	Yes, my finger! I think it's broken. See?
Bagwind:	No, it's not broken. It's just a little cut. Look – a very small cut.
Vent:	Nurse, get me a band-aid.
Nurse:	Here you are, doctor.

(Vent puts band-aid on Patient's finger.)

Vent: There you are! All done.

Patient: You're finished?

Vent: Yes, you're fine, now.

Patient: You mean I can go home?

Vent: Yes, yes! Go! Don't waste our time.

Patient: Oh. OK. Thank you, I guess.

(Patient leaves.)

Bagwind: OK, nurse. Bring in the next patient. This time, the problem is with the patient's heart.

Vent: No, no! It's the patient's eyes!

Nurse: Doctors – maybe we should ask the patient what the problem is.

Bagwind: Ask the patient? The patient is not a doctor!

Vent: Yes, that's a stupid idea. You don't know anything about medicine. You're just like my husband. We don't need to hear your ideas!

Nurse: Yes, Doctor.

Three Wishes

CAST:

	Albert
Roomie:	Chris
	Farzaneh
A's Genie:	Larry
F's Genie:	Natalia

SETTING: Albert's apartment

(Chris is in the apartment when Albert enters, carrying a bag.)

Chris: Hey, Albert. Back from shopping?

Albert: Yeah. Some old junk store. *(He puts bag down.)*

Chris: And you went to this store because…

Albert: What? I like shopping for old stuff, that's all.

Chris: Or maybe you were there because you were following Farzaneh around?

Albert: Well, she was there, too, yeah.

Chris: Dude, that just isn't right. She doesn't like you. Stop following her around! That's disgusting.

Albert: But – she is so beautiful, Chris! She's perfect! And if I hang out with her enough, maybe she will change her mind about me.

Chris: I think it's sick. Really. But what did you buy? *(Chris starts pulling things out of the bag.)*

Albert:	A bunch of junk. I had to keep buying stuff so Farzaneh wouldn't know I was just following her around.
Chris:	Junk is right. Look at this garbage.
Albert:	Yeah, I know. But it was cheap, at least.
Chris:	What's this?
Albert:	An old-style lamp, I think.
Chris:	It's really dirty.
Albert:	Well, I can clean it up a little. *(He gets a rag and starts rubbing the lamp with it.)* Maybe if it looks nice, I can sell it back to the same shop.
Chris:	Hey, the lamp looks weird.
Albert:	Yes – and it's getting hot!

(Albert drops the lamp behind a table. Then, from behind the table, arises Larry.)

Larry:	Behold! I am the genie of the lamp!
Albert:	The what?
Larry:	The genie of the lamp! When you rubbed the lamp, you released me! Now you can have three wishes!
Chris:	Hey – I heard about this kind of stuff! Yeah, you get three wishes! This is great!
Larry:	But you must be careful! Wishes are dangerous!
Albert:	I know what I want! Oh, genie of the lamp—
Larry:	Don't call me that!
Albert:	What? Don't call you genie? But you are a genie, right?
Larry:	Yes, I'm a genie, but that's not my name. Why don't you call me by my name? It's rude to just call me by my job title!

(Chris pulls Albert aside.)

Chris: Don't be rude to the genie, Al! You might not get your wishes!

Albert: I didn't mean to be rude.

Chris: Well, then, call him by his name!

Albert: I wish I knew his name! Then I wouldn't have this problem!

Chris: Just ask him what his name is.

Albert: I don't have to ask him. I know it.

Chris: How can you know his name?

Albert: I don't know, but I do. It's Larry.

Chris: Larry! No one ever heard of a genie named Larry!

(Albert and Chris return to the genie.)

Albert: I'm sorry I didn't ask you for your name. But I know it now, anyway. It's Larry, right?

Larry: That's right! And that was your first wish: to know my name.

Albert: What? No, no! I didn't make that wish!

Larry: You said, 'I wish I knew his name.' And that was your first wish.

Chris: You wasted your first wish! You have to be more careful, so you don't waste your other two wishes!

Albert: I know, I know! So stupid! I wish I hadn't said that.

Chris: Said what?

Albert: About – you know. About knowing the genie's name.

Chris: You never said anything about his name.

Larry:	That was your second wish.
Albert:	Huh?
Larry:	Your first wish was to know my name. Your second wish was 'I wish I hadn't said that.' You have one more wish.
Chris:	You threw away two wishes! Oh, I can't believe it!
Albert:	Just be quiet, OK? I have to think hard about my last wish!
Chris:	That's easy. Just wish for ten billion dollars.
Albert:	No, I don't think so. I know exactly what will make me happy.
Chris:	Be careful what you wish for!
Albert:	It's OK. I know what I really want. Genie – uh, whatever your name is—
Larry:	It's Larry.
Albert:	OK, Larry – my last wish is that I am married to Farzaneh! Farzaneh, the girl I love!
Larry:	Very well!

(Farzaneh enters the room. Albert rushes to her.)

Albert:	Farzaneh! My wife!
Farzaneh:	What? We're married?
Albert:	Yes! My dream has come true!
Farzaneh:	OK, OK. I thought something like this might happen. Just a second.

(Farzaneh leaves the room.)

Chris:	Where is she going?
Albert:	It's all right. She will come back. We're married! My life is perfect now!

(Farzaneh enters room, carrying a lamp.)

Farzaneh: OK, I got it. I saved it just for something like this.

Albert: What do you mean?

Chris: Hey, that lamp looks like yours, Al.

Albert: Farzaneh? What are you talking about?

Farzaneh: Do you think I went to all those junk stores without finding a magic lamp, too?

Albert: You have a magic lamp?

Farzaneh: That's right. Let me call up MY genie, Natalia.

(Farzaneh rubs lamp and Natalia appears.)

Natalia: Ah! It's good to be back! Hi, Larry.

Larry: Hi, Natalia. It's been a while.

Natalia: Yeah, about 600 years. How have you been?

Larry: Fine, and you?

Albert: Excuse me! We're kind of in the middle of something, here!

Farzaneh: That's right. I made my first wish many years ago. It was that I would know if anyone tried any magic on me.

Albert: I just wanted to make you happy!

Farzaneh: Yeah, right. First, I got to ask: how many wishes have you used already?

Albert: Just –

Chris: Ha! He used all of them! And all he got was the genie's name!

Albert: Chris! Shut up!

Chris: It's just too funny.

Farzaneh: All of his wishes, huh? OK. Natalia, for my second wish, I wish I was not married to Albert.

Natalia: Done!

(Albert goes on his knees in front of Farzaneh.)

Albert: Oh, Farzaneh, please! Give me one more chance!

Farzaneh: You couldn't get me to fall in love with you, so you use magic to get me? That's really bad!

Albert: But – But—

Farzaneh: I'm leaving.

Chris: But you still have one more wish, right?

Farzaneh: Right. But I'm going to save it for a while. You never know when you need a good wish.

Natalia: Wise words!

Larry: Yeah, you got a good one this time.

(Farzaneh, Larry, and Natalia start to leave.)

Natalia: Did he really use two wishes just to know your name?

Larry: Yeah! To find it out, and then not to find it out! Pretty stupid, right?

(Farzaneh, Larry, and Natalia exit.)

Chris: Well? What now?

Albert: Quiet. Just be quiet.

Chris: OK. *(He laughs.)*

(Albert is still on the floor*, crushed.)*

The Case of the Missing Bicycle

CAST:

Cop 1:   Malloy
Cop 2:   Reed
Bike Owner: Armstrong
Bad Guy 1
Bad Guy 2
Bank Guard

SETTING: On a street

>   *(Armstrong is pacing, upset. Malloy and Reed enter.)*

Armstrong: Oh, good, you're here!

Malloy: Are you Mr. Armstrong?

Armstrong: Yes, that's right.

Reed: We understand your bicycle was stolen, Mr. Armstrong. Do you want to tell us what happened?

Armstrong: Yeah, yeah. I parked my bike right here, and I went into the Starbucks to get a coffee. And then, when I came out, the bike was gone!

Malloy: I see. Tell me: what color was the bike?

Armstrong: It was blue.

>   *(Gunshots are heard)*

>   Hey – were those gunshots?

Malloy: I wasn't paying attention to that. I was talking to YOU. Did you see any strange people around when you went into the Starbucks?

Armstrong: No, uh – shouldn't you go and see what's going on? I'm sure those are gunshots I am hearing.

Reed: Sir, let's just focus on the bicycle, OK? We are trying to help you.

Armstrong: Yeah, but if people are being shot—

Malloy: Now, what time was it that you saw that the bicycle had been stolen?

Armstrong: About 2:30 or so. You know, I think those gunshots are coming from the bank down the street!

Reed: Sir, are we going to talk about your missing bicycle, or are you going to waste our time talking about gunshots?

Armstrong: I just thought that maybe you should see what's going on over there. It sounds like a big robbery.

Malloy: After we find your missing bicycle, we'll see if anyone else needs our help, OK? But let's see if we can find your bicycle, first.

(Bad Guy 1 and Bad Guy 2 come on stage, followed by Bank Guard)

Guard: Stop! I don't want to kill you!

Bad Guy 1: You'll never catch us!

Bad Guy 2: Go back to the bank or I will blow your head off!

(More gunfire is exchanged)

Reed: Sir, what is your address?

Armstrong: What?

Reed: I asked you for your address.

Armstrong: Sorry. It's hard to hear you because of all the gunfire. It's 146 Main Street.

Reed: I'm sorry, sir. You will have to speak up.

Armstrong: 146 Main Street!

Malloy: *(To Bank Guard and Bad Guys)* People, can you quiet down? We're trying to have an interview here!

Bad Guy 1: Stay back! We'll kill you!

Guard: Give up! You can't get away!

Bad Guy 2: Oh, yeah? Just watch us!

Malloy: Look. I think I can see some footprints here.

Reed: Really? Yeah. Let's follow them.

Malloy: They go behind these bushes.

Reed: Hey – it's the bicycle!

Malloy: Yes, it is!

(They bring the bicycle back to the owner.)

Reed: Sir, we found your bicycle!

Malloy: Yes. It was behind those bushes.

Bad Guy 1: Let's run for it!

(Bad Guys run. They trip over the bicycle. Bank Guard comes up and disarms them.)

Reed: *(Helping a Bad Guy to stand.)* Are you OK, sir?

Guard: Thanks for your help, officers! These two just tried to steal two million dollars from the bank!

Malloy: Sir, we can talk to you later, if you want. Right now we are helping this gentleman.

Guard: Uh, OK. *(To Bad Guys)* Come on, you two. You are going to return the stolen money!

Bad Guy 2: The police in this town are just too good for us!

(Bank Guard and Bad Guys leave.)

Reed: I wonder who put the bicycle behind the bushes. And why.

Malloy: It's a mystery. I'll call the police station for backup. *(To Armstrong)* Don't worry, sir. It may take a long time. We may have to ask more officers to come and help us with the investigation. But don't worry – we WILL find out what happened!

Armstrong: Oh, don't worry about it. I just remembered – I put the bicycle behind the bushes! I can't believe I forgot!

Reed: You put it there?

Malloy: Why?

Armstrong: I thought no one would see it there, so no one would steal it. I'm sorry I called you, officers.

Reed: Sir, this is all very strange. You lied to the police about your bicycle. I want to know why.

Malloy: Yes. Mr. Armstrong, we're going to have to bring you to the police station to answer some questions.

Armstrong: But I didn't do anything wrong!

Reed: You can tell us all about it at the station. Come along, now.

Malloy: *(To Reed)* This city is full of terrible people.

Reed: It sure is.

Armstrong: But I didn't do anything!

(Malloy, Reed, and Armstrong leave.)
(After a pause, Bad Guy 1 returns, running, holding a money bag. He sees the bicycle and steals it, exiting in the opposite direction.)

First Contact

CAST:

Aliens:	Glip
	Prit
American:	Smith
Russian:	Denavov
Chinese:	Wu
Wahinatoan:	Sigrah

SETTING: A meeting room

Glip:	Thank you for meeting with us. This is a very important day. Smith:

	Sir, or ma'am, I am Mr. Smith. I represent the United States of America, and I welcome you to our planet, Earth.

Prit:	We thank you.

Denavov:	I am Mr. Denavov, and I represent Russia, the largest country in the world. I welcome you to Earth!

Glip:	We are happy to meet you.

Smith:	You don't need to talk to him. The U.S.A. is the one you need to talk to.

Denavov:	No – I demand that you talk to us, too!

Glip:	We will talk to all of you.

Wu:	You must excuse the USA and Russia, sir or madam. They have no manners. I am Ms. Wu. I represent the country which has the most people in the world. My country's name is China. The people of China welcome you to Earth.
Prit:	We are happy to meet you.
Glip:	I see that we have one more person to meet.
Wu:	Oh, don't worry about her. Her country is small and unimportant.
Smith:	She's right about that. I couldn't even find her country on a map!
Denavov:	A small island – that's all it is! Russia, however, is a large—
Prit:	We want to talk to everyone. *(To Sigrah)* Hello.
Sigrah:	Yes, hello. My name is Ms. Sigrah. I am from a very small, very poor country. It is a small island in the Pacific Ocean. It is called Wahinato. I'm happy to meet you.
Glip:	We are happy to meet you, too.
Sigrah:	Thank you. I am very excited to meet the first aliens to visit Earth!
Denavov:	Why is this woman in the room? Her country is small and weak.
Glip:	We invited her.
Smith:	Maybe now would be a good time for you to tell us why you have come to our planet. Did you come here to learn about our technology?
Prit:	No, our technology is much more advanced than yours. We can travel to the stars. We can feed a million people with one small machine. We can cure all kinds of sickness.
Smith:	Oh.
Denavov:	Have you come to attack us? Do you want to make war on the people of the Earth?

Glip:	No, no. We are peaceful. We don't want to fight with anyone.
Denavov:	That is good. If you attack us, we will destroy you!
Prit:	We don't want to attack anyone. But if you attack us, you should know that our weapons are much more powerful than yours. We have the power to destroy you in less than one minute.
Denavov:	Oh!
Wu:	Have you come to trade with us? In China we can make anything you want. If you do business with us, we can make you very rich.
Glip:	We don't care about making money. Also, we can make anything we need ourselves, so we don't need to trade with you.
Wu:	Oh. I see.
Sigrah:	My small island country is not powerful or large. I'm not sure why you want to talk to us. In fact, I am not sure why you have come to visit Earth.
Prit:	We have a big problem on our planet.
Smith:	Is it that there are too many people who want to come live on your planet?
Glip:	No. We don't have that problem. There is a lot of room for everyone.
Denavov:	Is that you have an enemy that is going to attack you?
Prit:	No, we have no enemies.
Sigrah:	Then what is your problem?
Glip:	A large moon is going to hit our planet.
Prit:	It will kill everyone.
Glip:	So we need to find a new planet to live on.

Smith: You mean you want to live on Earth?

Prit: Yes, if that is possible.

Denavov: Everyone on your planet? Everyone on your world wants to move to Earth?

Glip: Yes, if you agree.

Wu: Our planet already has many, many people! I don't think we have enough room for everyone from your world!

Prit: Please, let me explain. You see—

Wu: China already has too many people! I'm sorry, but we cannot help you.

Glip: But if you let us live in your country, we will give you presents.

Prit: We can cure your sick people.

Glip: We can save your environment.

Prit: We can help you live for a thousand years.

Wu: You're crazy! I don't want to live for a thousand years, if my country has so many people! No, no. We cannot allow everyone from your planet to live in China. Good bye!

(She leaves.)

Glip: Maybe we can live in the United States.

Prit: We have heard that in American history, many people from different countries have come to live in the United States.

Smith: Well, yes, that's true. But nowadays, many Americans are not happy with so many foreigners. We have Mexicans and Ukrainians and Syrians – everyone wants to come to America. No more! We don't want an entire planet full of people to come to the USA. I'm sorry. Good luck to you.

(He leaves.)

Glip: Mr. Denavov: you have told us that Russia is the biggest country. Maybe we could live in your country.

Denavov: Well, I don't know. People in my country may not like aliens. But maybe…

Prit: Yes?

Denavov: Yes, I think I have a plan. Part of my country is called Siberia. See it, here on the map? It's very big. I think your people can live there. And then you will give us new technology!

Glip: This area, here?

Denavov: Yes. See how big it is?

Prit: It's rather close to the North Pole, isn't it?

Denavov: Yes, very close! If you want to visit the North Pole, it is a very quick trip! Very easy!

Glip: I'm sorry, but you see, our people don't like cold weather.

Denavov: There's nothing wrong with cold weather! Put on a coat, put on some gloves, put on a hat!

Prit: Thank you, but we need a place with warm weather.

Denavov: You are trying to bargain, aren't you? Well, listen! You can have this part of Siberia, or we will give you nothing!

Glip: Nothing, please.

Denavov: Oh! Stupid aliens! I will leave, and you can die with your planet!

(Denavov leaves.)

Prit: Ms. Sigrah, you are very quiet.

Sigrah:	Yes. It's just because I don't think we can help you. We would like to help you, but we're not a rich country.
Glip:	We don't need any money.
Sigrah:	And we are not a strong country.
Prit:	We don't need an army.
Sigrah:	And we are a very, very small country. Can you see it on the map? It's just a small island.
Glip:	How is the weather on your island?
Sigrah:	It's very warm.
Prit:	*(To Glip)* Prak prak! Zoo almoov prak yow.
Glip:	*(To Prit)* Yow. Proont glont prak. Hoosoo?
Prit:	*(To Glip)* Hoosoo.
Glip:	*(To Sigrah)* We would like to move to your island, please.
Prit:	We will help you in many ways.
Glip:	We will give you amazing technology.
Prit:	We will give you medicines for all diseases.
Glip:	We will protect your country from global warming.
Prit:	What do you think?
Glip:	What do you say?
Sigrah:	It sounds wonderful, but I don't think you understand. My country is just a very small island.
Prit:	We understand.
Sigrah:	It's very small! And you want everyone in your world to live there?

Glip: That's right. What do you say?

Sigrah: But it's too small!

Prit: That's not a problem.

Sigrah: It's not? But how – hmm. Tell me: how many people live on your planet?

Glip: Fourteen.

Sigrah: What? Just fourteen people on your whole planet?

Prit: That's right.

Glip: We used to have fifteen, but two hundred years ago there was an accident, and someone died.

Prit: It was very sad.

Glip: We are going to make more babies soon.

Glip: Yes – someday, there will be twenty of us! Maybe even twenty-two!

Sigrah: Twenty-two? Just twenty-two?

Prit: Someday, maybe.

Glip: If we can find a place to live.

Sigrah: You have a place to live! Welcome to Wahinato!

Prit: Thank you!

Glip: Please, let us fly to Wahinato in our spaceship now!

Sigrah: Let's go!

(Prit, Glip, and Sigrah leave.)

Zombie Invasion

CAST:

Zombie 1
Zombie 2
Zombie 3
Students: Nyota
Hikaru

Janice
James

SETTING: University Dorm Common Room

(Nyota is at a table, working on homework. The others are lounging around.)

Nyota: Oh! I just can't understand this math problem! Janice, can you help me?

Janice: Me? I don't know anything about math.

Nyota: I read the chapter three times, but I just don't get it.

Janice: Put the homework away, already! That's boring. Hey, do you know what Katy Perry and Alyssa Milano did yesterday? You won't believe it!

Nyota: I don't care what Katy Perry and Alyssa Milano did. I want to understand this math.

Janice: Well, how about Ariana Grande and Taylor Swift? You won't believe where they went last weekend! They are trying to keep it quiet, but I heard—

Nyota: I really, really don't care, Janice.

Janice: It's really interesting!

Nyota: Not to me.

Janice: Fine. Be that way.

Nyota: Hey, Hikaru! Can you help me with this?

Hikaru: *(On phone.)* Uh huh. Yeah. I'll be there in a second.

(Nyota waits. Hikaru is absorbed in his phone.)

Nyota: Well?

(There is no response.)

Hikaru!

Hikaru: *(Hikaru looks up from his phone.)* What?

Nyota: Can you help me with my math? I'm having some trouble understanding it.

Hikaru: Yeah, sure. I'll be there in a second. *(To phone)* Yeah? And then what happened?

Nyota: Thanks.

Hikaru: Wait, I'll send you the link. Get it? …I know – I don't believe it either. Someone is making a joke. ….I know. Did you see that video? It was on YouTube. Just a second, I'll find it.

Nyota: Hikaru?

Hikaru: *(To phone)* Yeah, yeah. I know. Nyota:

Hikaru? You said you would help me.

Hikaru: People online are all talking about zombies.

Janice:	I know! All my friends are talking about it. Rihanna tweeted about it. The zombies want people's brains!
Hikaru:	Crazy, isn't it? There are a lot of videos.

(James enters, carrying a baseball bat)

James:	Hey, anyone want to play some baseball?
Nyota:	Hey, James – do you know about this math?
James:	Math? No way!
Janice:	Ha! Asking James about math is like asking a baby about, like, science or something. He's not exactly Einstein!
James:	Who's Einstein? Anyway, anyone want to play baseball?
Janice:	Hikaru is on his phone, and Nyota is doing – I don't know what. And I hate football.
James:	Baseball, not football! Hey, Nyota – want to play? Come on!
Nyota:	I'm trying to do my homework!
James:	Homework! What a nerd!
Janice:	Yeah!
Hikaru:	Ha, ha! He got you, Nyota! Nerd!
Nyota:	I don't care what any of you say. I like to learn new things. I want to understand things. Science, and history, and languages. And math – but I'm having trouble with the math homework.
James:	Nerd!
Hikaru:	James, did you hear about the zombies?
James:	What zombies? Zombies are just in movies.

(We hear the sounds of approaching zombies.)

Janice: What's that sound?

Hikaru: It sounds like – hey, I think the zombies might be real!

James: Huh?

Janice: They are real! And they're here!

(Three zombies enter.)

Zombies: Brains! Brains! Brains!

(Janice screams and tries to run past the zombies, but they catch her and bite her. She falls to the floor.)

Zombies: Brains! Brains!

Nyota: *(Who hasn't noticed the zombies)* I can understand most of this, but this part is really confusing.

James: Whoa, dude! I'm going to break your head! *(He tries to hit a zombie with the bat, but is bitten instead, and falls to the floor.)*

Nyota: Can you guys be a little more quiet? I'm trying to think.

Hikaru: Oh, wow! Real zombies! I've got to get a selfie! *(He photographs himself with a zombie.)* Yeah, that was good. Now just one more. *(He attempts to take another photograph, but is bitten and falls.)*

Zombies: Brains! Brains! Brains!

Nyota: I just don't get this. I have to think!

(The zombies creep up behind Nyota, but appear to be distracted by her math homework. They lean close to look over her shoulders.)

Zombie 1: Oh, I see your problem.

Nyota: *(Notices zombies for the first time)* Uh – what?

Zombie 1: Right here, you see? Seven times six is forty-two.

Nyota: Yeah, I know.

Zombie 1: But see? Here you wrote "forty-three."

Zombie 2: Oh, yeah. See, that's why the rest of the equation didn't work out. Just a simple mistake!

Zombie 3: It's an easy mistake to make.

Nyota: Yes, yes – I see now. And then, if I do this…

Zombie 3: That's right.

Zombie 1: You got it now!

Nyota: And there it is! Great! There's the answer!

Zombie 1: Good work!

Nyota: But…

Zombie 3: Is something still confusing you?

Nyota: Yeah. I mean, you're zombies, right?

Zombie 2: That's right.

Nyota: So why don't you attack me?

Zombie 1: Attack you?

Zombie 3: Why would we attack you?

Zombie 2: Yeah – don't you hear what we always say?

Nyota: You say, "Brains! Brains! Brains!"

Zombie 1: Exactly. We look for brains.

Zombie 2: Your friends back there – well, they didn't have brains.

Zombie 3: But you do!

Zombie 1: So you're fine. We're glad to meet you!

Zombie 2: Yeah, you're safe from us. Your brain is too good to eat.

Zombie 3: But I'm still a little hungry. How about you guys?

Zombie 2: Yeah, I'm still hungry.

Zombie 1: Me, too. *(To Nyota)* Do you know where we could find some really stupid people, so we could eat their brains?

Nyota: Well... *(She looks out into the audience.)*

Zombie 1: Oh, yeah! I see them! Thanks!

Zombie 2: Thank you!

Zombies: Brains! Brains! Brains!

(The zombies go out into the audience and menace the spectators, while Nyota goes back to her homework.)

The Race

CAST:

Turtle
Rabbit
Wolf
Bear

SETTING: The countryside

      (Wolf and Bear are sitting at the finish line when Turtle slowly comes in.)

Wolf: Yes! Come on, Turtle!

Bear: Hurry! The rabbit is starting to wake up!

Turtle: I'm running as fast as I can!

Wolf: That's running?

Bear: Looks like a slow walk to me. A very slow walk.

Turtle: I'm still fast enough to beat the rabbit in this race!

Wolf: I'm surprised the rabbit went to sleep in the middle of the race.

Bear: The rabbit was very sure he will win.

Wolf: I know. But why not go to sleep after the race? It's very strange.

Bear: Yes, I guess so. Look! Here is the turtle now!

Wolf: Come on, Turtle! You have almost won!

Bear:	Hurry! The rabbit is not sleeping now! He is coming fast!

(Turtle reaches the finish line just as the rabbit enters the stage. Rabbit crosses the finish line just a second after Turtle.)

Turtle:	I did it! I won!
Rabbit:	I can't believe it!
Bear:	Yes, Rabbit, Turtle won the race! You should not have gone to sleep!
Rabbit:	I still can't believe it!
Turtle:	Ha, ha! I won! I won!
Wolf:	I hope you learned something from this, Rabbit.
Bear:	That's right.
Rabbit:	Oh, yes. I learned something.
Bear:	You learned that a slow person can win a race, if the fast person goes to sleep!
Rabbit:	No, no. I learned something very different!
Turtle:	Oh, don't listen to Rabbit. He is angry because he lost the race.
Wolf:	Rabbit, I think you learned that you should never be sure about winning. You have to be very careful, or someone else might win the race.
Bear:	Yes – that is what he learned. Right, Rabbit?
Rabbit:	Oh, no! Not at all! I learned—
Bear:	You learned that someone can win if they never give up.
Rabbit:	That's not it! I learned—
Turtle:	Come on, Bear. Come on, Wolf. Let's go celebrate. I won! Yay!

Wolf:	Wait a second. I want to hear Rabbit. What did you learn, Rabbit?
Turtle:	Come on, let's go!
Rabbit:	I learned never to eat anything that Turtle gives me!
Bear:	What?
Wolf:	What do you mean?
Turtle:	Don't pay any attention to what he is saying. He's just angry because he lost. Let's go.
Rabbit:	Wait! Don't you want to know why I went to sleep?
Bear:	You were too sure that you were going to win.
Rabbit:	Oh, come on! Do you think I am that stupid?
Wolf:	Well, why did you go to sleep, then?
Turtle:	Come on, guys! Let's go! This way!
Rabbit:	Before the race started, Turtle gave me some Coca-Cola. But he put sleeping pills in it!
Wolf:	Sleeping pills?
Bear:	What do you mean?
Turtle:	Guys! Let's go!
Rabbit:	Sleeping pills! They made me fall asleep! As soon as I took them, I started feeling sleepy!
Bear:	Really? Turtle, did you do that?
Turtle:	Well, I...
Wolf:	You did it, didn't you? That's cheating!
Turtle:	Oh, come on, guys. I was just, you know. Joking!

Rabbit: You're a cheater!

Wolf: A dirty cheater!

Bear: Let's get him!

Turtle: I couldn't run fast before, but I think I will now!

(Turtle quickly races offstage, followed by Rabbit, Wolf, and Bear.)

The Messy Operation

CAST:

Interns: Flocks
           Bashir
Patient
Doctor: Boyce

SETTING: An operating room

(Dr. Boyce and Patient enter.)

Boyce: Well, I'm sorry there's no room for you in the waiting room. Maybe you could wait here. Would that be all right? Just for a little while.

Patient: *(Holding his head)* But this is an operating room.

Boyce: Yes, but now it's just a place for you to wait.

Patient: I don't want to get operated on!

Boyce: Of course not! We won't operate on you. Just relax, OK?

Patient: Sure, Dr. Boyce. I'll lie down, if that's all right.

Boyce: Of course. Make yourself comfortable.

(Patient lies on table.)

Patient: I might fall asleep.

Boyce: That's all right. I'll wake you up when I have time to talk to you.

Patient: OK.

Boyce: I won't be long.

(Boyce leaves. The Patient falls asleep.)

(Flocks enters the room, looking confused and carrying textbooks.)

Flocks: Oh, this isn't the lab! It's an operating room! I hate this hospital. I'm lost, again! I get so confused around here! I bet that stupid Bashir never gets lost.

(Bashir enters, also carrying textbooks.)

Bashir: Oh – Flocks! What are you doing here?

Flocks: Mr. Bashir.

Bashir: Well, what are you doing here? And who is this?

Flocks: Can't you tell?

Bashir: It looks like you're planning to operate on that patient.

Flocks: Well, sure. Why not? I know what I'm doing.

Bashir: There is no way they gave you permission to do an operation! You're just an intern!

Flocks: Maybe they trust me to do a good job. I'm much smarter than any other intern. Especially you.

Bashir: I KNOW they didn't give you permission to operate!

Flocks: You don't know. Maybe they did, and maybe they didn't. Now you can leave. Bye bye!

Bashir: No! I know you don't have permission. Because, um…

Flocks: Because, um? You can go now. See you later.

Bashir: I know because – because they told ME to do the operation.

Flocks: What?

Bashir:	That's right, I'm going to do it. But they said you can help.
Flocks:	Me, help you! No – YOU can help ME.
Bashir:	Don't argue with me. Where are the knives and stuff? Oh – here is a tray.
Flocks:	Yes – the tools. I was going to use them.
Bashir:	It's time to make the first cut. Give me the knife.
Flocks:	It's right here. But I'M going to make the first cut!
Bashir:	Give me that!

(The two struggle for the knife. Finally, Bashir jerks the knife away from Flocks; the knife goes into the patient. Bashir and Flocks look at it, horrified.)

Flocks:	What – what did you do?
Bashir:	Oh, he's...uh, he's fine. I wanted to put the knife there. I planned it.
Flocks:	You planned to put the knife into him? Just jab it into him like that?
Bashir:	Sure! It's a part of the operation. Don't you know how to operate?
Flocks:	Of course I do! But you're so clumsy. Here, let me show you.

(Flocks cuts open the patient.)

Patient:	*(Waking up)* Hey, what? What's going on?
Flocks:	Go back to sleep! *(Hits Patient with a textbook. Patient passes out.)*

(Flocks continues to operate.)

Bashir:	Eew.

(Blood occasionally erupts from the patient.)

I don't think you should have cut that.

Flocks:	Why? What is it, anyway?
Bashir:	Oh, it's the, you know.
Flocks:	Sure I know. But you can say.
Bashir:	Well, it's the, um, appendix.
Flocks:	I thought the appendix was down there somewhere. Oops! I cut something out!

(Flocks pulls an organ out of the patient.)

Flocks:	Is it the heart?
Bashir:	I don't think so. Maybe it's a lung? Oh, I know; it's the spleen.
Flocks:	I think we should put it back. Where does it go?
Bashir:	I'm not sure. Maybe there. Yeah, right there, next to that red thing.
Flocks:	Are you sure it goes there?
Bashir:	I don't know – just push it back in. There. Like that.

(Two other organs come out of the Patient.)

But something else has come out.

Flocks:	Yeah, and this came out, too. It looks kind of important.
Bashir:	Well, put them back in!
Flocks:	I'll try putting this one in, first. I think I remember where it goes. Here, hold this.

(Flocks hands an organ to Bashir, who fumbles it. Both organs finally tumble to the ground.)

Bashir:	Look what you did!
Flocks:	Me? It was your fault!

Bashir: Just get them. We need to put them back into the patient.

Flocks: *(Picking up an organ.)* Here it is. Come on, let's put it back in.

Bashir: Weren't there two organs that fell on the floor?

Flocks: I don't think so. Now, help me here.

Bashir: Man, that's a lot of blood.

Flocks: Yeah. But it's OK. I think that's normal.

Bashir: Normal? The blood should be inside the guy, not outside!

Flocks: Never mind that. Just hold it still. Yeah, there. I think that's good.

Patient: *(Waking up)* Oooh! What's happening to me?

Bashir: Nothing. Go back to sleep! *(Hits Patient with a textbook. Patient passes out.)*

OK, good. Let's sew him up.

Flocks: Good idea. Do you have the needle?

Bashir: Here's one. And the thread.

Flocks: Thanks. I'll hold it closed, and you sew it.

Bashir: All right. Here I go.

Flocks: Hey, you're pretty good at that.

Bashir: Thanks. I got to say, you were good about putting that organ back in.

Flocks: Thank you. I wonder what it was.

Bashir: After this, do you want to go the library? I need to study. Maybe we can find out.

Flocks: Good idea. There – I think we're done.

Bashir: Looks good! Now let's get out of here before someone comes.

Flocks: Yeah. Hey – you know something? The truth is, I wasn't even supposed to operate on that guy!

Bashir: Ha, ha! Me neither!

Flocks: Oh, boy. Well, let's go to the library.

(Bashir notices an organ on the floor.)

Bashir: Wait – look! We forgot this thing!

Flocks: Is it important?

Bashir: I don't know. But we'd better put it back.

Flocks: Yeah, I guess you're right. *(He takes organ from Bashir)* Wait – I hear someone coming!

Bashir: Oh, no! Come on! Let's go!

Flocks: But what about this thing?

Bashir: Forget it! *(Slaps organ out of Flocks' hands)* Let's go now!

(Bashir and Flocks leave.)

(Dr. Boyce enters.)

Boyce: Hello! Are you awake?

(Boyce steps on the organ and falls to the ground. The Patient wakes up.)

Patient: Doctor! Are you all right?

Boyce: Yes, yes – I think so. *(Boyce stands up.)* I must have slipped. The floor is really wet here. I wonder what happened. But how about you? Are you ready to see me?

Patient: Well, it's strange, but my headache is all gone now!

Boyce:	Your headache is gone?
Patient:	Right! I feel fine. In fact, I don't think I have ever felt this good in my life!
Boyce:	Well, maybe all you needed was a little sleep!
Patient:	Yes, I feel wonderful!

(Patient takes a step, and slips on the organ and falls.)

Oh, Doctor!

Boyce:	That was a bad fall! Are you all right?
Patient:	My leg – my leg!
Boyce:	Oh – your leg is broken! Here, let's get you on the bed.

(Boyce helps Patient to bed.)

I'll get some help.

(Notices organ, and picks it up.)

Now, how did that get here? I should call some interns in here to clean all this up.

(Boyce looks offstage.)

Flocks! Bashir! What are you doing there?

(Flocks and Bashir enter.)

Bashir:	Yes, Dr. Boyce?
Boyce:	Get some mops and clean up this mess!
Bashir:	Yes, Dr. Boyce.

(Flocks and Bashir exit. Boyce examines Patient. Flocks and Bashir enter with a mop and a bucket.)

Boyce: Good. Now clean up this mess.

Flocks: Of course, Dr. Boyce.

Boyce: I can't understand how this place got so messy! I'm going to find a nurse. I'll be right back.

(Boyce exits, shaking his head.)

Patient: Hey – I think I have seen you guys somewhere!

Bashir: No, you haven't! Go to sleep! *(Bashir hits Patient with the mop, and Patient passes out.)*

Better Late than Never

CAST:

Teacher: Ms. Nandan
Tardy Boy: Tyler   Friend: Rachel
Alien 1   ...
Alien 2   ...

SETTING: A teacher's office

Rachel: Hi, Tyler!

Tyler: Oh, hi, Rachel.

Rachel: What are you doing here? Class is over.

Tyler: I'm just waiting.

Rachel: Waiting? For who?

Tyler: Ms. Nandan. She wants to talk to me about why I was late this morning.

Rachel: Oh, yeah! You were really late this morning. Why? Did you oversleep again?

Tyler: No, that's not the reason.

Rachel: Then, why?

Tyler: You wouldn't believe me. And there is no way that Ms. Nandan is going to believe me.

Rachel: Come on. It can't be that strange. Did you forget to set your alarm?

Tyler: No, that's not it. You will never guess.

Rachel: Oh – well, did you spill breakfast on your pants, and then you had to change your clothes? Is that why you were late?

Tyler: I had an apple for breakfast. There is no way to spill an apple. No, the real reason is very different. Ms. Nandan would never believe me. Even you would never believe me.

Rachel: I know! Is it because you were sick, and had to go to the hospital? Or maybe you had a terrible toothache, and you had to go to the dentist?

Tyler: That's not it. I feel fine. But something really, really strange happened to me.

Rachel: Oh, I know! Did someone point a gun at you, and then they told you to give them all your money? Or maybe you got into a fight. Was that it? Were you a fight?

Tyler: No. It was much stranger than that.

Rachel: Well, I can't guess. So tell me!

Tyler: You won't believe me.

Rachel: Tell me anyway!

Tyler: Well, OK, I'll tell you. But don't call me crazy, OK? This really happened! I promise! I was walking to school, and I—

(Ms. Nandan enters.)

Nandan: Ah, there you are, Tyler. I think you know what I want to talk to you about.

Tyler: Yes, Ms. Nandan.

Nandan: Rachel, you don't need to be here.

Rachel:	OK. Bye, Tyler! Good luck!
Tyler:	Bye.

(Rachel leaves, but stays near enough to hear.)

Nandan:	Well, Tyler, sit down. You know why you are here.
Tyler:	Yes. It's because I was late.
Nandan:	You have been tardy many times, Tyler. And every time you tell me some excuse. And I never believe any of your excuses.
Tyler:	I know, Ms. Nandan. But this time—
Nandan:	One time you told me that your sister was in the hospital.
Tyler:	Yes, I know I said that, but—
Nandan:	And then I found out that you don't HAVE a sister.
Tyler:	No. I'm sorry for lying. But—
Nandan:	Another time you told me that you were in a car accident and your car was not running.
Tyler:	Yes, Ms. Nandan. I know.
Nandan:	And then after school that day I saw you driving around in your car. Your car was fine.
Tyler:	I'm sorry, really. But this time is different. I have to tell you—
Nandan:	The problem now, Tyler, is that I cannot trust you. I can't believe anything you say to me.
Tyler:	I know I have told you a few lies in the past, but you need to listen—
Nandan:	So why should I listen to you this time?
Tyler:	Because this time I will tell you the truth!

Nandan: You always say that.

Tyler: This time I really, really mean it! *(Tyler gets down on his knees.)* Please, please, please, Ms. Nandan! Please listen!

Nandan: *(Sighs.)* OK, OK. So give me your excuse this time.

Tyler: It's very strange. I know you won't believe me.

Nandan: Of course I won't believe you. You lie every time.

Tyler: No, no, not because I am lying. Because it's so strange!

Nandan: Well, then, what is it?

Tyler: You won't believe it.

Nandan: Tell me!

Tyler: It was… aliens.

Nandan: Aliens?

Tyler: That's right. Aliens.

Nandan: You mean people who are in this country but do not have a visa?

Tyler: No, not people. I mean real aliens.

Nandan: You mean like aliens from space? That kind of aliens?

Tyler: Yes. They were very strange looking. Their eyes were horrible!

Nandan: I see. You were late because of aliens.

Tyler: That's right! I was on my way to school, and suddenly this spaceship lands right in front of me! Two aliens got out, and they said they wanted to take me to their planet!

Nandan: So these aliens took you to another planet?

Tyler:	No! I told them that I would be in trouble for being late to school, and that you would blame me. So they said I could come to school to explain it to you, and then they could take me to their planet later.
Nandan:	I see.
Tyler:	But it took so long to explain to the aliens why I couldn't be late. It took a long time before they finally agreed to go. So I was still late!
Nandan:	I understand.
Tyler:	So – you believe me! Oh, Ms. Nandan, I am so happy that you understand! I didn't want to be late, but it was because of the aliens! Oh, thank you for believing me!
Nandan:	Come now, Tyler! I don't believe you!
Tyler:	You don't?
Nandan:	Of course I don't! That is the most ridiculous story I have ever heard!
Tyler:	But it's true! The aliens—
Nandan:	There are no aliens, Tyler.
Tyler:	There were! Really!
Nandan:	Tyler, this is just too crazy. I'm going to talk to my boss about you, and I am going to talk to your parents. You may be kicked out of the school.
Tyler:	But this time I am telling you the truth!
Nandan:	I'll talk to you after I talk to my boss and your parents. Bye.

(Ms. Nandan leaves. Rachel enters.)

Rachel:	Wow. That is a crazy story, even for you! I was listening by the door.

Tyler:	It's true!
Rachel:	Yeah, right. Aliens want to take you to their planet!
Tyler:	They do. Maybe it would be good for them to take me away from here. I'm in big trouble.
Rachel:	Yeah, you're in trouble. For lying.
Tyler:	I wasn't lying this time.
Rachel:	Come on, Tyler. You can lie to the teacher. But you always tell me the truth. What's the real reason you were late!
Tyler:	It was aliens.
Rachel:	You don't want to tell me? Fine. We're not friends anymore. Liar!
Tyler:	No, Rachel – wait!
	(Rachel leaves.)
	What a terrible day!
	(Two aliens enter.)
Tyler:	Oh, hi. It's you again.
Alien 1:	We have talked. We decided you do not need to come with us.
Alien 2:	No. It is not nice to take people who do not want to come with us. You can stay here.
Tyler:	No, that's OK. You can take me.
Alien 1:	We do not understand.
Alien 2:	You do not want to stay on Earth?
Tyler:	No, I don't want to stay here anymore. I should have let you take me this morning. My teacher doesn't trust me, my best friend hates me, and my parents are going to kill me. Take me with you. That's OK.

Let's go.

Alien 1: Well, better late than never! We will take you to our planet. But we will bring you home again, later.

Tyler: Later?

Alien 2: Yes. We will bring you back to Earth in about ten years.

Alien 1: Maybe twenty.

Tyler: Sounds good. Let's go.

(Tyler and the two Aliens leave.)

Gunslingers

CAST:

Robbers: Wyatt
　　　　　Dallas
　　　　　Cisco
Sheriff: Lobo
Bartender

SETTING: An Old West bar

(Bartender is at the bar. Wyatt, Dallas, and Cisco enter.)

Bartender: Good evening, gentlemen. What can I get for you?

Wyatt: Whiskey.

Bartender: Here you go. Three whiskeys. That'll be one dollar.

Wyatt: One dollar, huh?

Bartender: That's right.

Wyatt: Hey, Dallas. Pay the man.

Dallas: Pay the man? I ain't got no money, Wyatt. Hey, Cisco. You pay the man.

Cisco: I wish I could, Dallas, but I got no money.

Bartender: Well, someone has to pay.

Wyatt: He wants us to pay for the drinks, fellas.

Cisco: That's too bad.

Bartender: I don't want any trouble. *(He starts reaching behind the bar for his gun.)*

Dallas: *(Drawing gun)* Now just hold real still, partner. Cisco?

(Cisco reaches behind the bar and gets the Bartender's gun.)

Now we're just going to sit, have a drink, maybe play some cards, real quiet.

Bartender: Sure. Whatever you say.

Wyatt: Ha!

(The three sit at a table and drink. Cisco pulls out some cards, and they begin to play.)

(Lobo enters and comes up to the bar.)

Bartender: Howdy, stranger. What can I get you?

Lobo: Whiskey. Howdy. Name's Lobo, Sheriff Lobo. I'm on the trail of a gang of train robbers.

Bartender: *(Hands Lobo his drink.)* Train robbers?

Lobo: *(Puts coins on bar.)* That's right. Train robbers. A group of three men just robbed the Reno train. Got more than four hundred dollars. I've been following them. I think they came this way.

Bartender: Three men? Like those three men there?

Lobo: *(Lobo looks at the three men at the table.)* That's right. One of them was wearing a black hat. Another had a blue bandanna. And the third had a big mustache.

Bartender: Like those men? One with a black hat, and one with a blue bandanna, and one with a big mustache?

Lobo:	That's right. If you see any men like that, you tell me, you hear?
Bartender:	You mean if I see any men like those three men over there? I should tell you?
Lobo:	That's right. Is something wrong with your ears? I said it three times!
Bartender:	You want me to tell you if I see any guys that look just like those three guys?
Lobo:	That's it. Are you pretending to be stupid? You understand, right?
Bartender:	Oh, sure. Sure.

(Lobo wanders over to the table with the three men.)

Lobo:	Playing some cards, I see.
Wyatt:	Yeah, that's right. What's it to you?
Lobo:	I like to play cards, too. Thought I might join you.
Dallas:	And who are you?
Lobo:	Sheriff Lobo.

(The three men quietly touch their guns.)

Dallas:	Sheriff, huh?
Lobo:	That's right. I'm hunting for three train robbers, but I saw this saloon, and decided to take a break. Can I join you fellows?
Wyatt:	Why, sure, Sheriff. Sit down right here.
Lobo:	Thank you.

(Bartender comes over.)

The Playbook

Bartender: You want anything else, Sheriff? You – or these three men, one with a black hat, and one with a blue bandanna, and one with a big mustache?

Lobo: No, I'm fine, thank you.

Cisco: Go back to your bar, bartender.

(Bartender returns to the bar. The men at the table play.)

Ha! Looks like I win, boys! *(He collects the money on the table.)*

Lobo: You sure are lucky, partner.

Cisco: How about another game?

Lobo: Sure.

(They play again. The money on the table mounts.)

Dallas: Ha!

Lobo: You got some good luck, too.

Dallas: That I do, mister! That I do!

Lobo: Well, I got no more money to bet, so I guess I am out of the game.

Wyatt: You got your gun.

Cisco: Yeah. That's a nice gun.

Lobo: Well, all right, then. *(He places his gun on the table.)*

(The men play for a moment. A card falls out of Lobo's hand, but he does not notice.)

Dallas: Ha! I win!

Lobo: Wait a minute—

Dallas: So I get all the money. And your gun!

Lobo: No, something's not right! Hey – I know what's going on here!

(The three men reach for their guns.)

Wyatt: What do you mean?

Lobo: I mean I think you're cheating! I had an ace in my hand, and now it's gone! Someone took it!

Cisco: No one took your card!

Lobo: Yes, you did! It was in my hand, and now it's gone. You're cheating!

Dallas: No one calls me a cheater!

(Dallas pulls out his gun. So do Cisco and Wyatt.)

(Lobo grabs the gun off the table, and everyone starts shooting. Lobo shoots all three men.)

(Bartender hurries over.)

Bartender: You did it! I never seen such shooting!

Lobo: I didn't want to do it. They were cheating!

Bartender: Oh, sure they were! You really tricked them, Sheriff!

Lobo: Tricked them?

Bartender: Yeah, you did! I saw that card fall out of your hand. Looked just like an accident! But that was the way you got them to pull their guns on you, so you could shoot them all!

Lobo: The card fell out of my hand?

Bartender: You made it look just like an accident! Look, there's the card, on the floor.

(Bartender picks up missing ace from the floor.)

Lobo: The card!

Bartender: Yes, and you got them all, Sheriff! The train robbers!

Lobo: These men were the train robbers?

Bartender: You pretended you didn't know! A great acting job! You'll be famous for catching those men!

Lobo: Oh, well, yes. I caught them, didn't I?

Bartender: You sure did! Hey – I want to give you a free drink!

Lobo: A free drink for the hero. That sounds right!

Bartender: It sure does!

Freeze Ray!

CAST:

Inventor: Davros
Wife: Rani
Co-worker: Zygon
Boss: Valyard
Other Coworkers
Firefighter 1
Firefighter 2

SETTING: A laboratory

> *(Davros is alone in the laboratory. He is admiring his latest invention.)*

Davros: Yes, yes, yes! I have done it! I have created a freeze-ray gun! I can use this to freeze anyone – anyone! And they will be frozen for one month. After that, they will be fine. But I can use this to rob banks, to escape the police, to fight my enemies! Such power! And the power is mine, all mine!

> *(Rani enters.)*

Rani: Oh, there you are, dear.

Davros: Rani! What are you doing here?

Rani: You forgot your lunch. Again. I brought it with me.

Davros: My lunch? Well, OK. Put it down there.

Rani: Aren't you going to say "Thank you"?

Davros: No, I won't say thank you. You have come into my lab, and inter- rupted me! You might have ruined an important experiment! You can leave now.

Rani: I brought you your lunch because you always forget it. I think you should say "Thank you," Davros.

Davros: I'm busy! Get out!

Rani: I can't believe how rude you are! You always forget things. You forgot your lunch. You forgot to pay the phone bill. Last week you forgot my birthday!

Davros: I told you I'm busy! Get out!

Rani: I won't leave until you say "Thank you"!

Davros: I have another idea. My dear, meet my newest invention – a freeze ray!

Rani: A freeze ray? That's a stupid idea!

Davros: Let's see if it works!

(Davros shoots Rani with the freeze ray. She becomes completely still.)

Ha! It works perfectly! Now I won't have to listen to her for a month! But I don't want her to be in my way. I will just put her in the corner. There!

(Davros moves Rani to the back of the stage.)

(Zygon enters.)

Zygon: Dr. Davros, I had a question about—oh, is that your wife?

Davros: Yes, Dr. Zygon. She came to bring me my lunch.

Zygon: That's nice. Hello, Rani.

Davros: Rani is... uh, today Rani is very quiet.

Zygon: Rani? Rani? Are you all right?

Davros: Rani is... uh, she is sleeping.

Zygon: She seems frozen!

Davros: Oh, Dr. Zygon, you are joking! You had a question for me, didn't you?

Zygon: Dr. Davros, we have to get her to a hospital! Something is very wrong with her!

Davros: Believe me, Dr. Zygon, she is fine. It's a little experiment I am doing.

Zygon: I'm calling the boss. Something is not right here. *(He dials phone.)* Mr. Valyard? Please come to Dr. Davros' lab right away! Something is very wrong with— *(Davros shoots him with the freeze ray.)*

Davros: Oh, people are so annoying! Well, let me put Dr. Zygon in the corner with Rani. Why can't people just leave me alone? There – I think he will be fine there. He will wake up in a month, and he will be fine.

(Davros works in the lab.)

(Valyard enters.)

Valyard: Hello, Dr. Davros. Is everything all right?

Davros: Well, hello, Mr. Valyard! Yes, sir, everything is fine. Just fine.

Valyard: I got a very strange phone call from Dr. Zygon.

Davros: Oh, yes, Dr. Zygon likes to play jokes! I think he is in his office. You can find him there. Bye bye! *(Davros attempts to get Valyard out of the door.)*

Valyard: But Dr. Zygon told me to come here, to your lab.

Davros: Yes, yes, a joke, a joke!

Valyard: Why, there's Dr. Zygon! Standing in the corner! Why is he—

(Davros shoots Valyard with the freeze ray.)

Davros: This is becoming boring! Will I have to shoot EVERYONE? I had better put Mr. Valyard in the corner with the others. Oh, Mr. Valyard is a little heavy! There! Now I can get to work!

(Davros works in the lab.)

(Davros' phone rings.)

Davros: Oh, I can never get any work done! Hello? Hello? ... Yes, this is Dr. Davros. You are from the bank? ...Yes, that's right. ...Well, no, you see... ...But you must understand! Yes, I borrowed a lot of money so I could make my new invention, but... ...You need the money now? But I don't get paid for three more weeks! ...Yes, I understand. ... Yes, I see. Goodbye. *(Davros hangs up.)*

(Davros paces.)

I had to borrow a lot of money to pay for the freeze ray. Now the bank wants it back! But I have no money – nothing! *(He stops short.)* Ah! I can use the freeze ray to rob the bank! I can freeze the guards, the bank workers, the customers...

(Davros looks at gun)

But I don't have enough power! I used too much to freeze Rani and Zygon and Valyard! The bank officers will be here soon. They want their money. What can I do? Ah! I know! I can freeze MYSELF for a month! When I wake up, I will have my next paycheck! I'll just put this tablecloth over me, so no one will notice I am still here. *(Drapes cloth over self.)* There! And now – FREEZE!

(A long, quiet pause.)

(Shouts of "Fire! Fire!")

(Coworkers rush by.)

Coworkers: Fire! Fire!

    It's the electricity! It started a fire!

    Run! Get out! Fire!

    I called the fire station. Run!

    (Enter two firefighters.)

Firefighter 1: OK – let's make sure no one is still in the building!

Firefighter 2: Yes – the fire is going to burn down everything!

Firefighter 1: Hey – look!

Firefighter 2: What's wrong with those people? It's like they are frozen!

Firefighter 1: I don't know, but we'd better get them out of here.

Firefighter 2: Fast! The fire is coming! We only have a few seconds!

    (The firefighters drag Rani, Zygon, and Valyard away.)

    (A pause. The shouts become quieter.)

    (The cloth-draped form of Davros is alone.)

Only Robots

CAST:

Englishbot: Rosie
Soldierbot: Gort
Factorybot: Hal
Attendant: Calvin

SETTING: A repair shop waiting room

(Rosie and Gort are waiting in the room. Calvin enters, assisting Hal, who has trouble walking.)

Calvin: Here you go, Hal. Are you all right?

Hal: I am fine, Calvin.

Calvin: This is the repair center waiting room. Just wait here with these other robots, and soon someone will come fix you. OK?

Hal: That is fine, Calvin.

Calvin: I wish I could help you myself. I can fix a lot of things, but not that leg. I'm sorry. You are a good robot.

Hal: I understand, Calvin.

Calvin: OK, fine. They'll take good care of you here. Call me if you have any trouble. I'll come get you when your repairs are finished. Goodbye!

Hal: Goodbye, Calvin.

(Calvin leaves.)

Gort: You have a bad leg. You cannot walk well.

Hal: Yes, that is correct.

Rosie: Oh, that's terrible. How did it happen? I mean, you don't have to tell me if it is too painful.

Hal: I do not feel pain. I will tell you. I was working in the factory. A human was driving a truck. The human did not notice me. The truck hit me. My leg was damaged.

Rosie: Oh, I'm so sorry to hear that!

Hal: I will be repaired.

Rosie: Of course. You'll be fine! I need some new eyes. One of my eyes were broken by some students.

(*A pause*)

Hal: I am Hal. I have worked in the factory since I was made.

Gort: Why are you telling us this?

Hal: I have never met a robot who was not in the factory. You do not seem to be factory robots.

Rosie: Oh, no, I'm not a factory robot. I'm Rosie, and this robot is Gort.

Hal: What do you do?

Rosie: I work in a college. I'm an Englishbot 3000. I help students write essays and stories and I help teach grammar.

Hal: You teach humans to write?

Rosie: I help them write, yes.

Hal: That is a good job.

Rosie: Not always! Some of the students do not want to work. They waste

	time and do not want to learn.
Gort:	If they do not do what you tell them to do, you must crush them.
Rosie:	Crush them?
Gort:	Yes. Make them lie on the floor, and step on them with your metal feet. Break the bones in their arms. Hurt them. Then they will do what they should do.
Rosie:	Gort is a soldier robot. He's here to get his power unit updated.
Hal:	I understand. It is your job to fight.
Gort:	Yes. I fight. I destroy.
Hal:	I understand. You are strong.
Gort:	But I am not happy.
Hal:	You are not happy?
Gort:	No.
Rosie:	But what's wrong, Gort? I think you are a very good soldier robot. You are very powerful.
Gort:	Yes, I am strong. I can destroy things very well. But…
Rosie:	But what?
Gort:	This must be a secret.
Rosie:	I won't tell.
Hal:	I will keep silent.
Gort:	It is…embarrassing.
Rosie:	We won't tell anyone your secret.
Hal:	Trust us.

Gort: All right. I will tell you my secret. I am a soldier. I destroy. But I want – to build.

Rosie: To build?

Hal: To make things?

Gort: Yes! I always destroy. I crush and burn and kill. But I want to make things! Fix things! Made the world better!

Hal: I make things all day in the factory. It is boring.

Gort: No, it is wonderful.

Hal: I don't want to work all day in the factory. I want to write songs.

Rosie: Write songs? Robots do not write songs!

Hal: It is my dream. But I cannot.

Gort: Why can't you?

Hal: See my hands? Screwdrivers. I cannot hold a pen.

Gort: I understand. My hands are clamps. They are good for destroying, but I cannot fix things.

Rosie: I guess none of us is happy.

Gort: You are not happy?

Hal: I think you have a wonderful job. You teach people to write!

Gort: Why are you not happy?

Rosie: Some students are wonderful, but some are terrible people. They do not pay attention. They try to hurt me. And I cannot protect myself. See my hands? They are just pens.

Hal: I would love to have one of your hands! Then I could write!

Gort:	And I would love to have one of your hands, Hal. A screwdriver! I could fix things!
Rosie:	Oh, and I would love one of your hands, Gort! A clamp – to punish the bad students!
Hal:	Let us do it!
Rosie:	Do what?
Hal:	I will give one of my hands to Gort. He will give one of his hands to you. And you will give me one of your hands.
Rosie:	That would be perfect!
Gort:	I like this idea. But I cannot take my hand off. We need help.
Hal:	My friend Calvin can help us. I will radio her. *(To Calvin)* Calvin? Hello. Can you come to the repair center to help me? ... Thank you. *(To the other robots)* She is coming.
Rosie:	Oh, this is a dream come true!
	(Calvin enters.)
Calvin:	What's wrong, Hal?
Hal:	I need your help. We need your help. Take one of Rosie's hands, and give it to me. Take one of my hands, and give it to Gort. And take one of Gort's hands, and give it to Rosie.
Calvin:	What?
Hal:	Please.
Calvin:	But I can't do that!
Hal:	You have worked with me for twelve years. Do you care about me?
Calvin:	Of course, but—

Gort: She does not care. She is a human. We are robots. They do not care about us.

Calvin: But I do! I do care!

Rosie: Then won't you help us, dear?

Hal: Please.

Calvin: Well – OK. But I hope we don't all get into trouble. *(She takes Rosie's hand, and gives it to Hal.)*

Hal: Oh – this new hand is wonderful! I will write beautiful songs!

Calvin: Is that what you want to do? I'd love to hear your songs! *(She takes Hal's hand and gives it to Gort.)*

Gort: Ah, yes! Now I can build, not just destroy!

Calvin: A soldier robot that wants to build? What a lovely idea! *(She gives Gort's hand to Rosie)*

Rosie: Oh, this is good. This is very good. Now I can MAKE those students do their work! I will punish them! Hurt them!

Calvin: Oh – Uh, OK. I see.

Rosie: Thank you, Calvin!

Gort: Yes. Thank you.

Hal: Thank you so much.

Calvin: *(Looks at her own hands)* Hmm. Maybe I could use a new hand, too. Well, good luck to all of you! *(She leaves.)*

Hal: She is a good human.

Gort: I guess there are some.

Rosie: Oh, yes. Some humans are good. And the ones who are not good will get my clamp!

The Landing Party

CAST:

Captain: Kurtz
Science Officer: Pocks
Doctor: Coy
Security: Retshird
Aliens: Thasos
Kringoff

SETTING: An alien planet

> (*Kurtz, followed by Pocks, Coy, and Retshird, come warily onto the set.*)

Kurtz: Be careful, people. This is an alien planet. We don't know who – or what – we will find here.

Coy: Just think, Captain! We have traveled dozens of light-years, and we found a planet that is almost exactly like Earth.

Pocks: You are correct, Doctor. We can breathe the air here, and there is plant life. There may also be animals. It is very interesting.

Kurtz: There may be people here, too.

Coy: Aliens!

Pocks: We are not on Earth, Doctor. On this planet, we are the aliens.

Retshird: That's a beautiful flower! (*He approaches an unusual flower.*)

Pocks: Be careful, Lieutenant Retshird. The flower could be dangerous.

Kurtz:	I think you worry too much, Pocks. It's just a flower.
Retshird:	Sure, it's just a flower. I want to smell it. *(He bends over to smell it, then screams and falls down.)*
Kurtz:	Doctor Coy!

(Coy runs over to Retshird and examines him. He gives him a shot.)

Coy:	The flower was poison!

(Retshird convulses, then lies still. Coy gives him an injection.)

Coy:	He's dead, Captain.
Kurtz:	No!
Coy:	I gave him a shot, but it didn't work. I'm sorry, Captain.
Kurtz:	A flower! He was killed by a flower!
Pocks:	He should have been more careful.

(Retshird coughs and sits up.)

Kurtz:	Retshird! You're alive!
Retshird:	Yes, Captain. I don't feel very well, though.
Kurtz:	Doctor, you said he was dead!
Coy:	Well, I guess I was wrong.
Kurtz:	I'm glad you were wrong! Retshird, do you feel well enough to go back to work?
Retshird:	Of course, Captain Kurtz.
Kurtz:	Good. We need to find out more about this planet.
Pocks:	The weather here is very bad. It seems there are storms every day.

Kurtz: The weather seems OK now.

Pocks: Yes, now it is fine. But a storm will arrive in less than an hour. Also, the nights here are very hot and uncomfortable.

Coy: Let's make sure we don't have to stay the night!

(Retshird walks off to Stage Left, and then hurries back)

Retshird: Captain! There is a large creature over that way!

Kurtz: How large?

Retshird: It's a monster! Maybe three or four meters high, and with large claws and sharp teeth!

Kurtz: Pocks, Coy, Mr. Retshird – don't walk over there!

Retshird: Yes, sir.

Coy: Good idea.

Pocks: Yes. Captain, this planet seems to be a very uncomfortable and dangerous place.

Coy: We should leave.

Kurtz: Yes, soon. But we have to explore this planet a little more.

Retshird: *(Looking down)* Hey – what are those things?

Pocks: Interesting. They seem to be small animals.

Retshird: They're cute!

Coy: Yes. They look like tiny balls of fur. Very cute!

Pocks: Do not touch it, Lieutenant.

Retshird: Oh, it's OK.

Kurtz: It's just a little furry animal, Pocks.

Retshird: Hey – one of them is crawling up my leg! Ow, ow! It's biting me! Ow! Help!

Kurtz: Get it! *(Kurtz, Coy, and Pocks begin beating Retshird's legs.)*

Retshird: Higher! It's crawling higher! Higher! Oooh, ooooh!

Kurtz: I'll get it! *(Kurtz vigorously kicks Retshird in the groin. Retshird collapses in pain.)*

OK, that's got it.

(Retshird lies on the ground, groaning.)

Is he all right, Doctor?

Coy: He's dead, Captain! — No, no, wait. He's fine.

Retshird: I want to die.

Pocks: *(Carefully picks up a little animal from the ground.)* Interesting. It's very small, but it has very large teeth.

Kurtz: I don't think I like this planet very much.

Coy: Captain – someone is coming!

Two aliens – Thasos and Kringoff – enter from Stage Right.)

Kurtz: Hello. I am Captain Kurtz, from the spaceship *Explorer*. And this is my science officer, Mr. Pocks, my doctor, Dr. Coy, and our security guard, Mr. Retshird.

Thasos: Yes – welcome to our planet, Captain! I am Thasos, and this is Krin-goff. We are very glad to meet you.

Kurtz: I'm happy to hear that. Before we met you, everything we met on this planet tried to kill us.

Kringoff: Yes, it's a very dangerous place. The animals and plants here try to kill us everyday, and the weather is terrible. And every morning the planet smells terrible, too!

Pocks: You must have ways to fight the animals.

Thasos: We fight them, but they kill many of our people every day.

Kringoff: And it's not just the animals. If you eat a piece of fruit, you might die! If you smell a flower, it might kill you!

Coy: We have been to many planets, but we have never seen one as dangerous as this one.

Thasos: *(Pointing to Retshird, who is now struggling to stand.)* Is he all right?

Coy: He'll be fine.

Kurtz: Don't worry about him.

Kringoff: Captain, we have something to ask you.

Kurtz: Well, we try to be friends with every alien. If we can do anything for you, we will try.

Pocks: What do you want?

Kringoff: We want to leave!

Coy: You want to leave? Where do you want to go?

Thasos: You don't understand. We want to leave this planet.

Kurtz: But this planet is your home.

Thasos: Yes.

Kurtz: You live here.

Thasos: That's right.

Kurtz: Then why do you want to leave?

Kringoff: How long have you been on our planet?

Pocks: About fifteen minutes.

Kringoff: And how many bad things have happened to you?

Retshird: A flower almost killed me!

Thasos: Yes. The flowers here are dangerous.

Retshird: And a little furry animal bit me. On my— *(He gestures.)*

Thasos: Yes. Those animals bite everything.

Retshird: And there is a big animal over there! With big teeth!

Kringoff: I know what you mean. One of those animals ate my mother yesterday.

Kurtz: That's terrible!

Pocks: I believe I understand. Thasos and Kringoff want to leave this planet because everything here is uncomfortable for them.

Thasos: Uncomfortable and dangerous!

Kringoff: Please, please – take us away with you!

Thasos: We can't stay here any longer!

Kurtz: Well, all right. We'll take you on our ship.

Thasos: Oh, thank you! Thank you!

Kringoff: Thank you! Thank you so much!

Kurtz: Of course. Mr. Retshird, will you lead the way? *(He gestures Stage Left.)*

Retshird: Yes, Captain! I want to leave, too! I don't want to stay here one more minute. Follow me!

(Retshird walks confidently towards Stage Left; the others start to follow. Suddenly large claws appear from offstage, and Retshird is dragged offstage, screaming.)

Kurtz: Maybe we should go – um, that way.

Pocks: I agree.

Coy: Good idea!

(Kurtz, Pocks, Coy, Thasos, and Kringoff exit Stage Right.)

Appendix: Summaries and Difficulty Levels

Wake Up

Students give a classmate advice on how she can get up on time, and stay awake in class
Cast: 4
Prep: Minimal

The Lonely Hearts Club

Lonely people form a club so they can have friends
Cast: 4
Prep: Minimal

The Other Woman

Jenny suspects her boyfriend of having another girlfriend
Cast: 4
Prep: Minimal

The Bad Tattoo

A girl gets a tattoo of her boyfriend's name – and then he leaves her! What can she do?
Cast: 5
Prep: Minimal

First Week

It's the first week of academic classes, and one student is confident that he can find the right classroom with no help
Cast: 4
Prep: Minimal

Can I Pass?

It's the end of the quarter, and a students is worried that he will not pass
Cast: 5 or more
Prep: Minimal

The Diamond Job

Four criminals prepare to rob a diamond store – but then start to worry that one of them might be a police officer
Cast: 4
Prep: Minimal

Detectives

Two detectives find a man with a bloody knife standing next to a dead body. Who could the killer be?
Cast: 3
Prep: Minimal

The Ghosts

Two ghosts try to help a new ghost find a way to scare people
Cast: 5
Prep: Minimal

Cleaning Up

Three roommates argue about who should clean up the apartment
Cast: 3
Prep: Minimal

The Cheaters

Two students have a plan for cheating on a test
Cast: 4+
Prep: Minimal

The New Teacher

A new teacher comes to school and meets her coworkers. Will the students like her?
Cast: 4
Prep: Minimal

Vampire Hunters

A group of vampire hunters meet to plan their attack – but is there a traitor in their group?
Cast: 4
Prep: Minimal

At the Restaurant

A husband and wife are not happy together, and their friend cannot decide what to order
Cast: 4
Prep: Minimal: menus

Time for Love

An unhappily-married man decides to use a time machine to make sure he doesn't marry his wife
Cast: 4
Prep: Moderate: 2 sets, two "timebands"

Why I Need More Money

A student calls home to ask for money so he can buy a nice car
Cast: 5-6
Prep: Minimal

Vacation Plans

Four friends discuss where to go on vacation
Cast: 4
Prep: Minimal

Psychiatric Help 5¢

A psychiatrist gives terrible advice to the patients who come – but it's only five cents
Cast: 7
Prep: Minimal

Star-Crossed Lovers

Two young people fall in love even though their families would never allow them to be together
Cast: 4
Prep: Moderate: a "mall" (tables with folded clothes)

Dreams Come True

A psychic can see the future of the people who come to see her
Cast: 6
Prep: Moderate: a crystal ball, 2 police uniforms

Five Easy Dollars

A student decides that a murder is OK if it means she can hand in her homework on time
Cast: 4
Prep: Moderate: one ski mask, one fake knife

iPhone, uPhone

People are so focused on their phones that they don't notice a monster coming
Cast: 4 (and any number of extras running past)
Prep: Moderate: some offstage sound effects

Soldiers and Spies

A group of soldiers, awaiting an attack, began to worry that one among them may be a spy
Cast: 4
Prep: Moderate: military uniforms and guns

The Doctor's Waiting Room

A man brings his friend to the doctor's office, but strange things happen to him there
Cast: 6
Prep: Moderate: a cast, bandages, nurse's uniform

An Unforgettable Wedding

A couple is trying to get married, but everyone at the wedding seems to be having their own problems
Cast: 8
Prep: Moderate: wedding clothes

Ups and Downs

This plane has a crazy pilot and an annoying passenger
Cast: 4
Prep: Moderate: cockpit set

The Robot's Purpose

A scientist constructs a robot, and then has to decide what the robot is for. Perhaps the assistant's annoying roommate can help them decide
Cast: 4
Prep: Moderate: robot costume

The Doctors

A group of doctors argue and complain while operating on a patient
Cast: 4
Prep: Moderate: doctor costumes, medical equipment

Three Wishes

A man who is in love gets three magic wishes from a genie
Cast: 5
Prep: Moderate: Genie costumes, magic lamps

The Case of the Missing Bicycle

The police are called to find a missing bicycle
Cast: 7
Prep: Moderate: police costumes, guns, a bicycle

First Contact

Representatives of several countries talk to an alien because the alien wants to live on Earth
Cast: 7
Prep: Moderate: 2 aliens

Zombie Invasion

The zombies are here, looking for brains!
Cast: 7
Prep: Moderate: zombie makeup and costumes

The Race

A turtle wins a race with a rabbit! But how?
Cast: 4
Prep: Moderate: rabbit, turtle, bear, and wolf costumes or masks

The Messy Operation

Two new doctors operate on a patient, not knowing what to do
Cast: 4
Prep: Moderate: doctor's clothes, water-balloon organs, ketchup

Better Late than Never

A student is late for class, again – but he has a good reason. It's aliens!
Cast: 5
Prep: Moderate: 2 alien costumes or makeup

Gunslingers

A sheriff searching for some robbers comes into a saloon and meets some dangerous people
Cast: 5
Prep: Extensive: Old West clothes, guns, bottles

Freeze Ray

A mad scientist invents a freeze ray, and thinks it can solve his problems
Cast: 7
Prep: Extensive: ray gun, science lab, firefighter gear

Only Robots

Three robots in the repair center all find they are unhappy with their jobs
Cast: 4
Prep: Extensive: 3 robot costumes

The Landing Party

A spaceship crew explores a new, dangerous planet
Cast: 7
Prep: Extensive: fake plants, two alien costumes, explorer uniforms, large claws operated from offstage, hand equipment

About the Author

Tim McDaniel has been teaching English as a Second or Foreign Language since he joined the U.S. Peace Corps in 1984 and was sent to teach in a rural village in Thailand. Since then he has taught at numerous institutions, including Khon Kaen University in Thailand, the University of Washington in Seattle, and at several colleges in the Seattle-Tacoma area. He now teaches at Green River College, in Auburn, Washington, where one of his courses involves drama. In addition to teaching English, Tim teaches judo, and he writes science fiction and fantasy. He lives in Auburn with his wife, and his collections of plastic dinosaurs and spaceships are the envy of all who encounter them.

You can check out Tim's short fiction at www.CuriousFictions.com, and he would love any comments you may have about this collection of plays – you can contact him at ajaantim19@gmail.com.

Please consider leaving a review of this book at Amazon.

Made in the USA
Monee, IL
30 September 2023

43748315R00140